The
KING'S CHOICE

The
KING'S CHOICE

You Only See My Beauty, But You Don't Know My Story

STACY AMEWOYI and THERESA LARYEA

XULON PRESS

Xulon Press
2301 Lucien Way #415
Maitland, FL 32751
407.339.4217
www.xulonpress.com

Unless otherwise indicated,Scripture quotations taken from the King James Version (KJV) – *public domain*.

Scripture quotations taken from New Life Version (NLV). Copyright © 1969 by Christian Literature International.Printed in the United States of America.

ISBN-13: 978-1-54564-320-4

Dedication

I dedicate this book to Rev. Joseph Lancelot Ammah-Tagoe of blessed memory.

Acknowledgements

I would like to first acknowledge God Almighty for his protection and provisions. I also acknowledge my family for all the love and support they have given me. I am thankful to my children for their patience during the times when I had to lock myself away to complete this book. Also, my sincerest gratitude goes to all those who supported me in diverse ways throughout my journey:

1. To my special and precious guardian angels.

2. Torgbui Azameti III of Global Reach, and GOFA Ministries

3. Dorcas Boamah

4. Terry O. Bright, Pastor Ray and Edward Kwashie Dodzi Amewoyi

5. Hayford, Ransford and Clifford

6. Mr. Omari and the Miracle Dancers, Mr Bandex and Ms Stella Yankey

7. Mr. Dada Kwaku Duah

8. Nana Quame

9. The Bekoe family, the Amewoyi family, and the Tagoe family in both Ghana and the United States.

10. The Governor, the Senyefia family and the Sintim Poku family

Table of Contents

Chapter One

Turbulent Arrival

The LORD will accomplish what concerns me; Your lovingkindness, O LORD, is everlasting; Do not forsake the works of Your hands. —(Psalm 138:8)

I was born on Sunday, the 26th of July, in the 1980s; but as to the accuracy of that date, I cannot tell. The only parents I have ever had were my grandparents and great-grandparents. I never knew my biological parents and only heard little bits and pieces about my mother. I heard that she was on her way to see the love of her life when I was born. I doubt that she kept me with her at all after I was born, because I know that she never breastfed me. I was born and bred in the dusty town of Bubiashie, near an old petrol station in Accra, Ghana. I began my education at the North 6 Primary School, popularly known as "Saito." I had a challenging time throughout my education; and as a result, my great-grandmother took me to a vocational institute to learn a trade. Food was hard to come by, especially with the number of mouths that had to be fed in the house. To fill my often empty stomach, I went around my compound house, looking for odd jobs to do. I pounded "fufu" (a dish made with yam, cassava or plantains); and washed peoples' clothes.

I was fortunate when some of my "customers" kindly gave me some of their used clothes, which even sometimes included underwear which I wore with gratitude.

Throughout Elementary School, I was always engaged in one fight or another, mainly because I was the one that stood up for the defenseless children who were being picked on by bullies. I can remember several major conflicts I was involved in. A girl who was blessed with long and thick hair but had a strong body odor was relentlessly picked on, and became the laughing stock of our class. Because of that, she intentionally skipped classes. One day, after school, I saw her crying and asked her what was wrong, and she told me about her ordeal. I marched her right back into the classroom and demanded to know who had made her cry. When the culprit confidently owned up, I beat him up until his face was bloodied, and I ended up getting suspended for it.

The second incident involved a gang of three boys who were engaged in voyeurism. They would use mirrors under their desks to view the girls' underwear. I located all three of them and gave them a good beating! As a form of punishment, I was locked up in the storage room of our school. Unfortunately, everybody forgot that I was in there and left for home after school closed. So I was left entirely alone in a dark and locked room on the school premises. It so happened that around that time, a spiritual phenomenon was taking place. It was an ongoing thing that had generated wide-spread hysteria in our school. It was rumored that a female teacher who had died after being beaten by her students was avenging her death. As the story went, her ghost would appear to her victims in red high-heels, tapping her feet. She apparently showed up in multiple schools. According to the rumors, if you heard the sound of tapping shoes and there was no one around, you were advised to take to your heels! I was terrified when I heard some footsteps which seemed to mimic the sound of high-heel shoes. My adrenaline shot up so high that I jumped from the window of the storage room which was on the second floor and ran all the way home! To think that I had to go through this traumatic experience all because I was defending the downtrodden!

All my antics earned me a reputation for being a rowdy and stubborn tom-boy. Our precarious financial situation forced me to be resourceful, so I plucked some mangos from the tree in the middle of our compound and sold them on the streets to generate some income with which to pay for my school fees. My great grandmother gave me a little container which I used to store the little money I made; it was through this that I learned how to save. Apart from selling mangoes, I also sold locally manufactured candies and cakes, popularly known as "Ayigbe Toffee" and "Kube Cake." Both of these were made from coconuts which I got from a tree in our compound. After plucking the coconuts, I grated them and dried them before I used them to make my cakes and candies. I sold my goods in school and used the proceeds to buy my lunch.

I enjoyed making money and loved to bring home some of my proceeds, irrespective of how little it was. I diligently worked hard to support my great-grandmother financially (God rest her soul.) She was such a noble woman who had never had any children of her own but took it upon herself to take care of her brother's children and grandchildren. She was a trader, but was not too successful, as she often got robbed. This led to the collapse of her business, so she had to work hard to make enough money to take care of our basic needs. There was a time when our financial state was so bad that I had no option but to drop out of school.

When I was in Class Six, I decided to work hard to pay for my school fees, school uniforms, and shoes. I decided to enter into the trading business by partnering with a lady who sold fruits which she brought from the village. I sold huge baskets of fruits after the close of school and gave her a percentage of my profits. Gradually, I added corn and plantains as well as different seasonal fruits and vegetables. This posed a significant challenge to my studies since I did not have time to study or to complete my assignments. I had to endure several lashes of the cane as my punishment. I believe that under much more favorable circumstances I could have excelled in my studies, but unfortunately, this was not the case since I had no structure at home. I also got punished for wearing crumpled clothes since we did not even own an electric iron. And though we had a box iron, I could not afford to buy the charcoal. I was also habitually late for school, which also got me punished. Our school uniforms had to be worn with black shoes and white socks, so I resorted to using the juice from batteries to polish my cheap Chinese shoes so that I could fit in and not be laughed at. The only thing that redeemed me was that I was an outstanding athlete and dancer, so I was able to help my school to win many medals at our interschool competitions. I did not come from a wealthy home, and I had no social standing and was often ostracized. Sometimes the people in my neighborhood would look at me and shake their heads, often telling me that nothing good would ever come of me.

In spite of the fact that my great-grandmother struggled to take care of me, she was filled with wisdom which she abundantly imparted to me. One of the things she advised me to do was to be hardworking and determined in all that I did. I followed that piece of advice and began to financially turn things around at a very tender age. I disciplined and trained myself to save my money. After a few months, I would go back to my piggy bank, which was either an empty milk tin with a small opening or a hole that I had dug in the ground; then I would take out what I had saved to buy all my basic needs. Another piece of advice that my great-grandmother gave me was never to cheat or allow anyone to cheat me under any circumstances. She also taught me to mind my own business. I often butt heads with the old lady, but she was the most constant figure in my life, and I am grateful that God gave her to me when I had no one else.

"When a human being is born, the first thing he does is to cry. The rest of his life he'll spend discovering why." —Erik Tanghe

Chapter Two

The Street Child

**"Give justice to the poor and the orphan;
uphold the rights of the oppressed
and the destitute. Rescue the poor and
helpless; deliver them from the grasp of
evil people." — (Psalm 82:3-4)**

I n spite of the fact that my great-grandmother took care of me, I could not escape the maltreatment and insults of other family members, who never ceased to remind me that I was an insignificant and illegitimate orphan. Their insults pierced my young heart and made me bleed inside. In a bid to escape the bullying and to find a means to earn more money, I joined one of my aunties at the "Kaneshie Market," where I helped her to sell some shrimps and onions during the school vacations.

When we went to the market, I secretly sold polythene bags on the side without my Auntie's knowledge, to make more profit. While trading, we also slept in the market with a sleeping area that was like a hen coop. It was a dorm packed with a full mix of people from the surrounding regions who had come to the capital to find greener pastures but had no place to sleep. The people who were from many different tribes sold various products like bread, polythene bags, fruits, and vegetables. There were also drivers, drivers' mates and all kinds of workers. It was a slum, each dorm full of between thirty and forty tenants who paid according to their financial capabilities. The sleeping areas were rented out based on a "first come, first serve" principle. We were crammed into the dorms, sleeping next to total strangers. Ventilation was almost non-existent, and I felt like I was suffocating on those hot nights. In the mornings, we paid for the use of the dirty public showers, and then we went out to work until night time.

Contrary to what you would think, I loved this lifestyle! It was not easy by any means, but it was liberating; and I was free from the insults and abuse from my family. I woke up at 5:30 am to do my "kayayoo" business; (a service rendered to the public by carrying their heavy loads.) I carried heavy goods like plantains and cassavas. I managed to collect the broken pieces from the foodstuffs, tied them together in a plastic bag and took them home for dinner. While I did my "kayayoo" business, I pinned my black polythene bags to my chest for sale. After selling my polythene bags, I went around looking out for the women who had come to Accra with snails and plantains to sell, and also helped them for a small fee.

I remember that there was a lady who brought some cocoyam to the market to sell on Tuesdays. Whenever she came around, I took a break from my "kayayoo" business and sold some of her cocoyam for her, giving an account of my sales at the end of the day. This was my life, hustling after my clients as a burden-bearer. Sometimes they asked me to go shopping for them, and I would scavenge around the market and find their goods in obscure places. Some of these clients paid well; others gave me a penny, and the rest paid nothing at all but whispered a quick "Thank You" or "God bless you." Whenever this happened, I was crushed and felt that I had been used.

In spite of my near destitute condition, one thing that God gave me in abundance was my natural beauty; I have a pretty face. Because of my good looks and my young age, people could not figure out what I was doing in the market. They could not understand why I was not in school or living under the watchful eyes of my parents. It was common for me to hear comments like, "Where is your mother? Why are you here alone? Whose daughter are you? Why are you on the streets and not in school?" I would smile at them, and say to myself, "You only see my beauty, but you don't know my story."

As time went by, the population at the Kaneshie Market increased as more and more youth dropped out of school or ran away from their homes. This affected the "kayayoo" business, as it became a matter of the survival of the fittest. In this case, the adage that the early bird catches the worm became literal. At this point, even the length of our slumber was cut short, and it was worse on the days when we were so many in a room. We had no option than to either queue in front of the stores, or sleep under a bridge; we also slept by the showers and the gutters. Though I stayed and worked in the market for such a short while, I managed to study the behavior of the people around me; how they spoke; how they slept, and how they related to other people. I also observed how they supported each other in love, and how united they were, and how they stood up for each other in spite of their poverty.

One of the stressful things about living in the market was the issue of security. There were times when I had my few belongings stolen, so I always had to have my luggage near me. Also, we were never sure of where we were going to spend the night. It is so sad that most families of runaway children are not aware of what they are doing on the streets in order to survive. Not all of them are there because of homelessness; they are there also because they are escaping from the abuse and ill-treatment of their relatives at home. They would rather fend for themselves amidst the danger on the streets than suffer a hellish existence at the hands of insensitive and cruel family members. Some of these children sadly end up as robbers and prostitutes; while others end up as housemaids who have to endure another kind of hell, like being maltreated by their employees, and sometimes even getting raped.

Life on the streets was like living on a battlefield! Most of us were starving and desperate to make enough money to buy our next meal. Extreme hunger can make you desperate; and desperation can cause you to do the most unthinkable things. If you were a lady and you were a deep sleeper, you risked being raped or attacked. You always had to have your wits about you, and you had to know how to defend yourself, so I often wore trousers or jeans to protect myself. I had to arm myself against the lethal mosquito bites by wearing socks on both my hands and feet. When school reopened, I went back home to my grandparents, but I continued to passionately pursue my business endeavors.

This time, I entered into the kerosene business, which I sold after school. One evening, as I plied my trade, I ended up wandering into a funeral party. There, I suddenly decided to throw caution to the wind and dance; so I danced my heart away, releasing my bruised soul to soar on the wings of the song. I got hooked on the feeling of ecstasy that comes from dancing. It thrust me into another realm in which I could escape (even though momentarily) from the sadness and emptiness in my life. I did not know that my exuberant dance had affected the crowd, until I heard them give me a thunderous applause. Right then, I had an epiphany! I could earn more money by dancing! So with that revelation, I entered into the dancing business, but I did so at a price.

Each time I told my grandparents that I was off to sell kerosene, I hid the fuel on the way and made a detour to where I was scheduled to dance. I made a tidy sum of money, and then went back for my kerosene. When I got home I gave my great-grandmother the proceeds from my dancing which she mistook as proceeds from my kerosene business. I hated deceiving her, but I knew that she would be extremely upset if she knew what I was doing; so I hid it from her. She was so happy about the amount of money I was making, that she eagerly took it without even bothering to find out how I was making so much money selling kerosene; neither did she worry about how late I was coming home. To show her appreciation and approval of how hard she thought I was working, by the time I came back home with the proceeds, she would have prepared my favorite dish for me, which was boiled cassava with pepper stew and "Keta School Boys" (fried fish.) Eventually, I quit selling kerosene altogether and focused solely on dancing; and I danced late into the night. This raised the suspicions of my great-grand-mother, who reported me to my older half-brother. He was my mother's son who was adopted by an uncle at a tender age to learn carpentry. We never really had a personal relationship because we did not live close to each other. However, once in a while he came home just to give me a beating whenever he heard that I had misbehaved. So it was no surprise to me when my great-grandmother reported me to him about my late night adventures; and I will never forget how mercilessly they disciplined me for it.

One night, I danced late into the night until I got home at around 2:00 am. As usual, I crept into my room and slid quietly into bed, only to suddenly feel the sharp and painful sting of a cane on my body. I jumped out of bed and ran to the door but it was locked. I turned around in the darkness and saw my great-grandmother's silhouette. She was holding a bowl in her hand. Then I saw with surprise that my brother was also in the room. They both grabbed me, and as I began to struggle, some of the contents in the bowl splashed into my eyes. It was ground ginger; and it painfully blinded me, as they tied me up and inserted the rest of the ginger into the most intimate part of my body, while they beat me mer-cilessly. I will never forget their brutality and the excruciating pain and shame that I suffered that night. What saddened me most was that no one in that big compound came to my rescue, as they all disapproved of my nocturnal activities. The pain was excruciating; I was in hell! I cried like I had never cried before, until I suddenly had an out-of-body experience. It is hard to explain, but I felt my spirit leave my body, as I hovered from above and watched the two of them beating me down below. Suddenly, I woke up to find myself being fanned, and water being poured all over me. I thought I would die from the pain, which was just too much to bear. My whole body was on fire; and I felt as though I had been skinned alive. I experienced hell on earth and lived to tell the story. My spirit was completely broken, my heart became as hard as a rock, and I became as stubborn and rebellious as ever.

Friends, never think that the more you beat a person, the better they become. In my case, the woman that I respected and trusted the most turned herself into my tormentor and ruined the one relationship I had treasured throughout my whole life. Never again did I trust her or any other person from that day forth. That fateful day, I lost all my respect for them. My brother had never enquired after me or extended any form of help to me throughout my schooling. All I received from him were beatings and insults. He never changed. All I needed in life was someone to care about me; someone I could confide in; and someone I could lean on; but I had no one. I was all alone in the world, fighting for survival. I cried out, but no one heard me or responded to my pain. Truly, the tears of the outcast are the hottest of all.

"You might be poor, your shoes might be broken, but your mind is a palace." —Frank McCourt

Chapter Three

The House Help

"Blessed are those who mourn, for they will be comforted." —(Matthew 5:4)

After God deemed it fit for me to survive that ordeal at the hands of my relatives, I decided to devote the rest of my life to explore my abilities to the highest potential. Success would be my greatest revenge. A restraint in me broke that horrific night; and though my family thought that they had reigned me in, they rather lost their hold and control over me. I decided that they did not deserve the privilege of having any say in my life anymore. It was their loss; and I felt sorry for them that they could not see the greatness that I knew was in me. My inhibitions gave way and my adventurous nature began to soar as I explored new things and new business endeavors. I fully embraced the fact that I was gifted with an entrepreneurial spirit and discovered that there was nothing I could not sell, and that I could make money off of just about anything. I can confidently say that there is nothing I have not sold before to date. Name them; I have sold them all.

In spite of the fact that I spent so much time making money instead of focusing on my studies, by the grace of God, I completed my Junior Secondary

School (now known as Junior High School.) I did not graduate with the best of grades, but with an aggregate twenty-one, I could quickly gain admission at a Senior Secondary School. At this point, no one in my family cared about whether I would continue my education or not, much less about how I would finance it. I was on my own, so I worked hard to gather enough money within the five-month break we had been given to prepare for admissions. I successfully managed to save some money to buy all the items on my prospectus. I paid for everything by myself; from my chop box to my scrubbing brush. I was packed and ready, and all I needed was an adult to go with me to register at the school. I also needed (old) GHC500, 000.00 (now GHC50.00) to pay my school fees, and sadly I could not find anyone to help me. My family believed that nothing good would ever come out of me, so they did not see it necessary to invest in my future. My great-grandmother would have helped if she could have, but at this point she had done all she could to provide for three generations, which included her brother's children, my grandparents and I, as well as other individuals that she had brought from the village. She was now well advanced in age and was not as strong as before. So I am sad to say that without the needed support, I had to miss the first semester of the academic year.

It was at this point that I genuinely felt the intense pain of not having my biological parents in my life. Here, I want to urge you that if you grew up with parents that loved you, protected you and provided for you, do not ever take them for granted. Be grateful to them and thank God for their lives. Also, if you come across children or youth like me, please do not abuse them or put them down. If you cannot help them, just let them be. It was so humiliating for me to have all my classmates going off excitedly to their new adventures, and leaving me at home with the younger children. I was mercilessly mocked and teased about not being able to go to school. The highlight of each day was when I visited the elderly tenants in my compound, because they were kind to me. They also enjoyed my visits, as I sat and watched television with them, providing for them a much needed companion. They were the only ones who showed any concern for my well-being. I remember one elderly tenant in particular; an old woman that everyone said was mentally retarded. Whether she was aware of it or not, she seemed to be the only one amongst the lot who had any pro-phetic insight about my potential and my future. She often addressed me as the "American Woman" and predicted that I would give birth to all my chil-dren in America. She encouraged me often and told me to ignore all the naysayers. There was also an elderly gentleman in the compound who used to tell me that I was going to be a great person and not to be discouraged by my surroundings or be affected by the negative perceptions of the people around me. He was confident of the fact that I would be great one day.

Unfortunately, I was too young and too discouraged to make any sense of what they were saying. I was overwhelmed by the harsh realities of my seemingly hopeless existence. After getting tired of being sub-jected to a constant stream of insults and mockery, I finally could not take it anymore, so I packed my few belongings and quietly left the house. I did not have a destination in mind, but I hoped to find some menial jobs along the way. My final goal was to find a permanent residence as a housemaid in a wealthy household.

The Maid in Distress

I became a sojourner, wandering around on foot for miles, from house to house, asking if people needed someone to clean their homes or wash their clothes. On three occasions, I had people who requested for my services, and I was able to get a job as a house-maid, but they were short-lived. I ran away because of the awful treatment I received at the hands of my employers. I slept very late after a hard day's work of washing, scrubbing, and cleaning. In one of the homes, every day I had to wait for the man of the house to return home from work, no matter how late, and wash his plates after he had finished his dinner. I ironed clothes, laid beds and filled bar-rels of water during seasons of water shortage. My only diet was made up of the left-overs of the chil-dren's meals.

My wakeup time was at 5 am, and when I overslept, I would wake up to cold water being poured over me or a painful slap on my body. Though I slept late, I had to wake up early. It was at this time that I began to understand the price of being light-skinned and pretty. I often had to endure harassment at the hands of the men in the houses. I even had a few of them spying on me while I showered. When I rejected their advances, I became their enemy so they would punish me for rejecting them. There were times when I was lied on and set up for crimes I did not commit. On more than one occasion, I was fired for no reason. Once, one of the men I had rejected .tore down clothes that I had laboriously washed into the mud, so that I had to rewash them. And as if that was not bad enough, I was extremely underpaid for my services.

In the last house that I worked in, my employment ended abruptly as I was beaten and forced out, without any money or even having the chance to pack my clothes. I left with tears streaming down my face, wearing a pair of blue slippers and the clothes on my back. This was because the man of the house had wanted to have an affair with me which I refused. And to get back at me, he told his wife that I had stolen money from his jacket when I did his laundry. His wife, without waiting to hear my side of the story pounced on me, beat me up and threw me out of the house. Later on, I found out that three other housemaids who came after me, all got impregnated by that same man, one after another.

There are always two sides to a story; so I encourage you my friends, to listen to both sides before you make your assumptions and judgments. After being kicked out of that house, I wandered about without realizing that I had walked for over two miles in about three hours. I entered another town and once again began asking people if they needed my services. As I proceeded on my rounds, I suddenly found employment in a restaurant. I could not believe my luck! I thought to myself, "Finally, I have found a resting place!" Little did I know what awaited me.

Before I was officially allowed to start work as a waitress, they required me to have a recommendation from a guarantor. I thought through my mind and wondered who would be willing to do this for me, but I could not think of anyone. Alas! I had no family member or friend who would willingly act as my guarantor. I continued to wander around until I met an elderly woman who struck up a conversation with me. I eventually found myself confiding in her; little did I know that she would one day be the cause of my downfall. I ultimately learned a hard lesson not to confide in strangers. In some cases, a stranger may be able to help you out, but in other situations, they might end up complicating your life and leading you on a path of regret. This lady told me that she had a niece who could allow me to impersonate her for a fee so that her niece's mother would go in and stand as my guarantor. As innocent and as desperate as I was, and seeing this as a good offer, I agreed. No one had ever taught me the importance of my identity or how dangerous it was to take on the identity of another person; especially a perfect stranger. The lady followed through and acted as my guarantor, and I finally got employed.

Gradually, things began to fall into place as I started working. The restaurant provided accommodation for its workers, so I joined the other female employees and lived with them in a dormitory. My physical stature at the time was more masculine than feminine, as I was just entering into puberty and was a little late in filling out. Except for my beautiful face, I could have easily passed as a male. I was light-skinned, very slim, with pink lips and a long pointed nose which I was told I got from my father who was of Malian descent. Because I had done so much manual labor in the past, I was stronger than I looked. My job at this restaurant was to pound "fufu." The size of the mortar and pestle was enormous! But I endured, and pounded every day, desperate not to go home empty-handed. Within a short time, I began to feel comfortable in my new workplace. I made new friends and made some more money from the tips I received. I eventually caught the eyes of the restaurant owners and was promoted to work in the "Big House." The "Big House" was the nickname given to the home of the owners of the restaurant. While working in the "Big House," I met their son who lived in the United Kingdom and had come for a visit. He took an interest in me and in no time requested for me to attend exclusively to him. I did his laundry and cleaning and even prepared and served him his meals. I enjoyed my assignment, as I became friends with him. In time, he wanted to take our friendship to the next level by marrying me, but I was not sure whether I wanted to be his wife or not, and I was still so young. His parents, upon hearing about their son's intentions surprisingly gave him their approval and support, and even went as far as to treat me with a greater level of kindness and respect while I diligently continued to discharge my duties.

Soon, news of my engagement got out, and my colleagues got wind of it. It was then that I understood the ugliness of the vice of envy. In life, rich men envy poor men, and poor men envy the rich; but in my case, the poor began to envy the poor! The senior female employees started to make my life a living hell, concocting all sorts of lies about me because they were upset that though I was the youngest among them, I had managed to catch the "Big Fish." It got so bad that they called me all kinds of names and did not even try to hide their hatred of me. I became afraid for my safety; after all, I shared the same room with these women, and they could easily gang up to harm me in the middle of the night. But little did I know that they were not my immediate threat, instead, someone else who I least expected.

"Sorrow looks back, Worry looks around, Faith looks up." —Ralph Waldo Emerson

Chapter Four

The Orphan's Cry

Father to the fatherless, defender of widows—this is God, whose dwelling is holy. —(Psalm 68:5)

O ne day as I was trying to figure out how to get out from under this unfair treatment, I heard someone wailing outside. I rushed out to go and see what was going on and got the shock of my life! The old woman that had provided me with a guarantor stood there wailing at the top of her lungs! By then, a small crowd had begun to form around her as people asked her what was wrong with her. I also curiously drew near to hear what she had to say. Nothing on earth would have prepared me for what was about to happen! Shockingly, I saw her pointing at me as she shouted, "She's a ghost! She's a ghost!" I looked at her incredulously and struggled to make sense of what she was saying. What on earth was this crazy old woman talking about? Then she began to tell her tale; and what a tall tale it was! According to her, she just received a phone call from someone who told her that her sister's daughter had been dead for two years, and I was that dead niece of hers who was now standing in front of them in the form of a ghost. I opened my mouth to protest and deny what she was saying,

23

but before I could get a word out, I received a hefty slap on my face! Then suddenly, my colleagues descended on me like an avalanche, slapping me in the face and kicking me all over my body. This was the opportunity they had been waiting for; this was their chance to unleash all their hatred and envy on me. I heard some of them angrily say as they brutalized me, "Oh yeah, that's why she's so beautiful! If she isn't a ghost, where did she get all that beauty from?" Now, I understand that we Africans are generally a superstitious people, but this was ridiculous! How could they believe such nonsense? Some of my colleagues even claimed that I hopped around in the bathroom each time I used it. One bizarre accusation after another continued to be leveled against me, until they grabbed me and tossed me into a room and locked me up. They reasoned that I would probably try to vanish if they left me outside. I will never understand how supposedly sane people could reason in such an insane manner! As I lay in agony bleeding on the floor, confused and in tears, I began to think back through my life, from my earliest childhood, throughout my Junior Secondary School until then. If I was a ghost, how did I feel so alive? Was I really a ghost? As crazy as it sounds, I began to believe that I was indeed a ghost, and even became terrified of my own self! It is a miracle that I did not go mentally insane through my ordeal!

The next day, the door of the room suddenly flung open, and I was roughly ordered to go outside. When I stepped outside, I realized that it was afternoon. There in the open, a crowd of onlookers had gathered, apparently waiting for my arrival. I was forced to my knees, and ground garlic and pepper was shoved into my mouth as I was forced to swallow it. This, according to them, was a ritual that would prove whether I was a ghost or a living human being. At that moment, I understood how desperately wicked and callous the human heart could be. Not even my pitiful condition, my swollen face or my tears could elicit even a tiny bit of compassion in the hearts of any of the women who stood around me. Instead, they all yelled at me to swallow the lethal concoction they had given me. This was just one of many tests they subjected me to, just to prove to them that I was not a ghost.

To prove that I was human, I told them where my family lived. So they roughly paraded me throughout the streets of "Awoshie" (a town in the capital) towards my family house in "Bubuashie." As I wept bitterly, I wondered what I had done in my life that was so bad that I deserved this kind of unending torment and humiliation. The crowd continued to hoot at me like I was a thief, all the way to my family compound. Finally, when we got to the house and my family confirmed who I was, and they realized that I was a human being and not a ghost, they took off, one after another, leaving me completely broken. They had proven my family right; no matter how hard I tried to make something of myself, I would never amount to much. I wept as though it was the last thing I would do on earth. I had so many unanswered questions swirling around in my mind; why had I been given this miserable life to live? Would it ever get any better? Was I under a curse? What was going to become of me? As I wept, I called out for my parents; my parents who had never cared for me a single day in my life. For days, I cried all day and all night; bitterness, rage, and sorrow threatened to swallow me up. It is a wonder I did not lose my sanity. I tried to think of someone in my life that I could go to who would console me. Alas! There was not a single person that I could go to for succor. The life of an orphan is a miserable existence and so full of sorrows that only another orphan can understand. Orphans are incredibly vulnerable, with no support and no defense, and are usually treated like the scum of the earth. I felt like a "nobody." I knew that if I were to have dropped dead, no one would have cared or mourned for me.

A while after my public humiliation, I heard that my fiancé (who at the time of my ordeal had gone to the UK for a two-week break) returned and met my absence. He immediately came to look for me, and I told him what they had done to me. He was livid! Though he tried his best to woo me back, I was so traumatized and embarrassed by what had happened that I had lost all interest in him and anything to do with him. No matter how hard I tried, I just could not get over it, so I let him go. Later on, I heard that in anger, he fired all the employees who had been at the restaurant during my ordeal. He packed his bags and went back to live permanently in the UK.

So once again I found myself in the same place I had tried so hard to escape. I was back in "Bubiashie," in my great-grandmother's house. After I recovered a bit from my ordeal, I decided to pick up the pieces and move forward; after all, I was still alive, and I needed to make a living somehow. So I set up a table in front of the house, decorated it with empty tins of milk, sugar, and Milo (a chocolate beverage) and began to sell them. By God's grace, I managed to get quite a bit of patronage for my business; but after a while, I felt like doing something different, so I decided to venture into hairdressing. I joined a salon as an apprentice, and in a year and six months, I was ready to graduate as a qualified hairdresser. I felt confident that life was now going to be so much better. But as usual, just when I felt like things were looking up, it seemed like a demon was sitting nearby, waiting for the least opportunity to trip me up or discourage me. Sadly, I heard that my biological mother had died. I have not spoken much about my mother until now because throughout my life I have only seen her twice, and it was for just a moment at each time. I remember when I was in Class Six in Primary School, a young lady came looking for my great-grandmother. She met me at the door and inquired of her, so I took her to her. After a short while, this same lady returned to me and asked me how I was doing, to which I replied that I was okay. She turned around and went to be with my great-grandmother for about thirty minutes, after which she left. It was then that my great-grandmother called me and told me that the lady that just left was my mother.

The next time I saw her again was when I was in JSS. One afternoon she came in, and this time she sat outside with my great-grandmother. I just stood at a distance looking at them without saying a word. After a few pleasantries were exchanged, she took off again. I did not hear from her until a few weeks to my graduation as a hairdresser when we were told that she was not feeling well. I made plans to visit her after my graduation which was two weeks away, so that I could get to know her better and ask her some questions about why she had abandoned me, but she decided to die on the day of my graduation. This was supposed to be one of the happiest days of my life. I was supposed to celebrate my emancipation, but instead, I was thrust headlong into mourning. I did not know that you could mourn a stranger; I mourned the mother I never knew. I grieved that she had never cared for me. I grieved not only because she was dead, but that she took along with her to the grave so many of the answers to the questions I had asked my whole life. And now I would never know, and I knew that I was truly alone in the world.

I felt so devastated, so once again I wept as bitterly as I had when I had suffered at the hands of the witch hunters. My family prepared for her burial, we had her funeral, and that was the end of it. Now, what was I supposed to do? The night after her burial, I sat under a coconut tree close to my house and sang mournful songs, crying out for the parents I had never known, and asking why they had left me alone in such a strange world. The depth of hopelessness that I felt cannot be described, and since I didn't believe in God, the emptiness I felt was profound. Indeed, without hope in Christ, life is an abyss of hopelessness.

I decided that since no one was willing to talk to me about my parents or give me any answers to my background, I would create a new life and identity for myself. So one day, I determined that it was time for the journey into my new life to begin. I thought that it would be a great idea to start my new adventure with a new name, because I figured that my old name had brought me so much bad luck. So I got a bottle of Coca-Cola, emptied it all over my head as a form of baptism, and repeated my new name over and over again. With the sound of the waves crashing on the beach and the leaves of the coconut tree rustling in the wind, I declared my entrance into my new life.

"When a mother dies too young, something inside her daughter always feels incomplete. There's a missing piece she continues to look for, an emptiness she keeps trying to fill."
—Hope Edelman

Chapter Five

My Blessed Mentor

Remember those who led you, who spoke the word of God to you; and considering the result of their conduct, imitate their faith. —(Hebrews 13:7)

As the Coca-Cola cascaded down my face, I decided to go all out with my little ceremony, so I prayed for the first time in my life. I told God that if He really existed, He should turn all the pain I have been through into something positive. I asked Him to give me the wisdom to be able to use my resources to help the poor and other people who were going through all that I had been through. This was by no means easy to pray, given my situation and all the things that God had allowed me to endure, but I managed to get it all out. After my "baptism," I was inspired and determined to make the best of my life. I went back for my old tea table and dusted it up; but this time I decorated it with hair creams and other beauty products which I received during my graduation. With that, I started my own hair salon. I did not have a hair drier yet, so I relaxed my clients' hair, set their hair in rollers and let them go home. They returned after a couple of hours of drying and I styled them. As time went by, my business did well, and I vowed to myself that after I broke even and made sizeable profits, I would remember to bless the less fortunate and become a voice for the voiceless.

Soon after, I made a friend who was also orphaned at a young age, and we became a team. My great-grand-mother gave us some space on the compound which used to house an animal shed. She advised me to save some money so that I could put up a structure for my hair salon. I took her advice, and by the grace of God was able to open a bank account. I then took out a loan and was able to put up a small structure. God was faithful and answered my prayers by enabling me to house a few homeless girls. Eventually, my salon became a haven in the community for anyone that needed to learn a trade in hairdressing. I did not take any money from the trainees but was able to fill my salon with all the driers and equipment necessary for its successful operation. I worked very hard and was able to pay off the loan within a considerably short amount of time. Gradually, I fully furnished the salon and even added a TV and a radio. I made sure to include every imaginable amenity that would ensure that my clients were comfortable. Sometimes I also served some of my clients meals, and they left looking beautiful and were full of smiles. I took customer service to a whole new level, and my clients left tremendously satisfied.

As I continued to prosper in my business, I remembered the pact that I had made with myself and God, that I would pour out to people all the things that I had been denied; and that I would pour out all the love, affection, attention and encouragement that I had missed throughout my whole life on others that needed it. Through word of mouth, I managed to capture a lot of clients and apprentices who came in from the capital and its outskirts. I was most ful-filled whenever I organized graduation ceremonies for my apprentices. To me it was an indication that I was indeed doing something worthwhile to ben-efit others. There was a depth of fulfillment that I received from this charity work that nothing else could duplicate, and I was deeply grateful that God had given me the means to fulfill this worthy vision.

Sometimes in life, God will send you someone that will impact you so greatly that they will change the whole trajectory of your life. Such a person blew into my life like a cool breeze and brought healing to my scarred and wounded soul. He was called Pastor Joseph Lancelot Ammah-Tagoe; a gentle, soft-spoken and genuine man of God who on a few occa-sions invited me to attend services in his church. By this time, I still did not know God or anything about the things of God. I reluctantly agreed to attend a service, not necessarily to please him or to seek an encounter with God, but to enjoy the snacks that I had heard they served the newcomers after ser-vice. On our way back home, Pastor Joe explained the sermon we had just heard and gave me some useful pieces of advice about life in general. I cau-tiously took it all in, because I was still a bit skep-tical about God. Pastor Joe was not fazed by my nonchalant attitude, but rather labored patiently with me until one day he broke through the walls I had erected for so long. On one of his visits, as he ministered to me, he said four words that changed my life and set me on the path to destiny: "I believe in you." The minute he said those words to me, it seemed as though a bright light shot through the thick darkness that had haunted me throughout my life. No one had ever told me that before. All they had told me was how useless I was, and that I would never amount to anything.

This reminds me of one world-renowned Pastor called Joel Osteen. Once, I heard him recount how he encountered a young man who joined him and a few friends to play basketball. This gentleman kept to himself and did not make any friends. Pastor Joel observed that as soon as the game was over, he would quietly vanish without a word to anyone. So one day after a game; he managed to quickly approach the man before he made his usual quick getaway. He smiled at him and gave him a pat on the back and told him it was always great to see him, and that he hoped to see him again. Game after game, this went on for a long time, until the man stopped coming altogether. Several years later, after Pastor Joel was well-established in ministry, a man walked up to him one day and asked him whether he remembered him. Pastor Joel could not place him until the man told him that he was the one who used to play basketball with him. Pleasantly surprised and intrigued, Pastor Joel decided to find out a little bit more about him. The gentleman told him his story; how those days when he came to play basketball he was going through a crisis. He told Pastor Joel how he came from a family that despised him and constantly put him down. However, he said the highlight of his life those days was when he came to play ball and Pastor Joel showed him such kindness and compassion. He said that it ministered greatly to him and gave him hope that something positive would come out of his life.

When Pastor Joe spoke those words of affirmation to me, I felt just like this young man must have felt. His words impacted me so much that I just broke down and wept bitterly. Those words broke the dam that I had erected for so long and healed me. My tears flowed copiously, until he asked me what he could do to help me. I told him I needed him to pray for me because I felt dry and empty. So he prayed and encouraged me until I felt like I could conquer the world! So with a new determination in my heart, I decided to work harder and seek God with all my heart. Pastor Joe, (may God rest his soul) demonstrated such compassion and unconditional love to me. There were times when I had so many clients lined up that I rather opted to work than to go to church. Pastor Joe would still come by after church, and without rebuking or condemning me, would go through the sermon with me. As the years went by, he continued to tutor me in the Word of God. He encouraged me to fast and pray on my birthday. The first time he told me this, I laughed in his face! Did he know who he was talking to? I had fasted my whole life, sometimes going for days without eating, and now I was independent and finally able to afford to eat anything I wanted, and he was telling me to willingly and intentionally go without food? He understood that I was spiritually immature and that I did not understand spiritual principles. He continued to persevere with my mentoring and on occasion took me to the beach where he gave me a list of prayer points to go through. He asked me to pray for my family, my future children, my future husband, and my destiny. As soon as he asked me to pray for my family, intense bitterness and offense flared up in my heart. Did he expect me to pray for the family that had made my life a living hell? And who told him that I ever wanted to get married? I loved my independence and was not about to hand it over to a man that would limit me. And I definitely did not want to have children, especially after the horrible childhood I had endured. So I wandered off to a corner of the beach a bit further away from him and pretended to pray. I did not understand that I was not deceiving him, but I was only deceiving myself. In spite of all these spiritual exercises, I found that I still lacked inner peace and joy. I had not surrendered wholly to God because I still had my defenses up and had not come to trust Him fully. One day, I suddenly had a burning desire to seek after God with all of my heart, so I got myself a Bible and went to church every day, opening myself up to everything that was taught. God responded in kind, just as He promised to draw near to anyone who draws near to Him. I began to experience the reality of God in my life as my devotional life intensified.

The next legacy that my mentor left me was the discipline of saving my money and not squandering it. All this while, I had not given up my part-time dancing engagements. I still loved to dance, and I was determined to have as many streams of income as I possibly could, since I still had to cater for the needs of my apprentices. By this time, I had graduated from dancing at funerals to becoming a professional dancer. I joined a dance group called the "Miracle Dancers" and this led me to land a part in a reality show called the "Embassy Club Pleasure." Being on the reality show set in motion a quick progression of events and caused me to relocate to a coastal town called Cape Coast which was three hours away from Accra. I got into cultural dancing and drumming, specializing in my favorite dance the "Bambaya" dance and drumming on the "Djembe" drums.

***A mentor is someone who allows you to see the hope inside yourself.* —Oprah Winfrey**

Chapter Six

The Dancing Queen

"For I know the plans I have for you,"
says the Lord. "They are plans for good
and not for disaster, to give you a future
and a hope." —*(Jeremiah 29:11)*

I continued on my path as a dancer, and steadily progressed as I diligently pursued my art. One day, I heard that there was an audition for dancers in Accra, so I went to audition for a spot. I was very excited when I was selected. I became part of a group of dancers who were hired to dance for some musicians. This was how I was introduced into the entertainment industry of Ghana. Though we were hired to perform at some events, we did not have a place to live, so we slept in a kiosk. Our caretaker, Mr. Omari- Oppong and his wife, Stella Yankey did the best they could to take care of us. Mr. Oppong saw in all of us great potential, and though we made very little income, he continued to encourage us and provided for us as best as he could. Unfortunately, some musicians kept disappointing him as they reneged on their payments, and this affected the quality of our upkeep. The little amount of money we made from competitions was used for our costumes. So in order to make ends meet, we had to go back to dancing at parties and funerals. There were times when we managed to get a contract to feature in some music videos. Some dancers charged exorbitant fees, but we were paid peanuts, yet we continued to labor in our craft.

Not too long after that, a friend from our dance group heard about auditions being held for a beauty pageant known as the "Miss Out of Gold pageant." She encouraged some of us to go and give it a try. When we got there, one of the judges saw me and picked me out, urging me to join in the auditions. He said that I was blessed with good looks and stood a chance of winning the whole pageant. This really boosted my confidence, so I determined to pursue it all the way. To my delight, I got selected for the pageant while my friend did not. I decided that I would not let her down and would win it for both of us. So I did my very best in every round and steadily progressed in the competition until I took the crown!

My position as "Miss Out of Gold" led me to great opportunities and exposure. I was seen on every television screen and lots of billboards, as I became the face of Akosombo Textiles Limited (ATL) and Da Viva (both textile companies). I also did an advert for Blue Jeans Energy Drink with the music trio, "VIP." Coupled with the exposure and contracts for billboards which earned me a lot of money, I was featured in music videos for secular and gospel artistes, as a dancer, as well as a backup vocalist. One Mr. Banda of "Bandex Production" saw the potential in me and decided to employ me, pushing me to work harder to excel in the industry. I then moved on to "Kaakyire Production" and worked with the musician Kaakyire Kwame Appiah, who became like a father to me. He empowered and supported all of us while we were under his mentorship. Another popular entertainer called Dada KD who was based in Germany also took me under his wings and advised me and gave me wise counsel concerning my future. Whenever he came down to Ghana, he made sure to check on me and took me along for all of his shows. He never took advantage of me or underestimated me. He was very sincere and generous to me, and I had a lot of respect for him.

I was also featured in several popular Ghanaian music videos which included "Bronya" with Kaakyire Kwame Appiah; "Lavender" with Slim Buster; "Wo Do Mu Ye Duru" with Tommy Wiredu; "Akusika" with Antwi ne Antwi; "Juliana" with Buddy Ro Ro and K2; "Siklitele" with 4x4, "Adofo Yeshia Shia" with Joe Frazier; "Antinga Bewe Atinga" with Nana Tuffuor; "Shake That Thing" by Okyeame Kofi and Okyeame Kwame; and "Indian Ocean" with Sony Achiba. I appeared in over 95% of the videos of the top musicians, and also acted with Agya Koo and Akroboto in some of the videos. At the same time, I went on live performances with Reggie Rockstone, Tic Tac, Abirekyieba Kofi Sammy, Screw Face, Pat Thomas, Papa Shee, Josh Laryea, Michael Dwamena, VIP, Batman (Samini), Ivy Stone, George Darko, Mzbel, Castro, Mary Agyepong, Abrewa Nana, Ex Doe, Nana King and other African artistes.

My experience with the musicians was a revelation in itself. In spite of their great talents, they managed their finances so poorly that they always seemed to be in need. Sometimes, just to gain more exposure, I worked for some of them, knowing that I would not get paid. On those nights, I came home to sleep on an empty stomach. The industry was not lucrative, but as long as I was doing what I loved to do, I was content. I will always be grateful for the kind of exposure it gave me. However one major drawback in my experience was that I had to endure some harassment by some of the musicians that I worked for, but God was merciful and kept me.

As time went on, I was blessed to cross paths with a gentleman known as Mr. Terry Ofosu Bright who was a video producer. He became a good friend and directed me to feature in some decent music videos. His entrance into my life was a great blessing to me. I enjoyed working with him so much that I quit all my other little performances so that I could commit to working entirely for him. He was very honest, sincere and generous to me. He never took advantage of me and treated me with the utmost kindness. This motivated me to work hard for him. A lot of us dancers will always be indebted to him and his assistant, Pastor Ray, who was also a great blessing to us all. Today, most of the dancers who benefited from his mentorship are well established all over the globe.

Dancing is the poetry of the foot. — John Dryden

Matters of the Heart

And now, let us take a little detour. At the age of seventeen, I entered into a relationship with a sweet and wonderful gentleman. He was one of a kind! My boyfriend never took advantage of me, as young and as naïve as I was. He took his time to get to know me, even when I tried to reject his advances. We met after I had won the "Miss Out of Gold" pageant. I remember that on the first day we met, he walked up to me and said that he admired my beauty and intelligence. He was impressed that I, a JHS graduate had stood toe to toe with women who were older and more educated than I was, yet I was the one that took away the ultimate prize. He happened to live right opposite the venue for the pageant, so each day he came in to watch the show with his friends. He asked me whether I would allow him to give me a "VIP treatment" and although I was scared, I accepted because of his warmth and charm. My boss, Mr. Omari, permitted me to leave with him in his car, along with my colleague dancers who had come to support me. He drove me all the way home, and that was how our love story began. He never told me that he loved me or got physical with me, but exhibited great care and kindness toward me.

He helped me out financially and always tried to talk me out of dancing. He saw the potential in me and thought that there were other things that I could excel at if I only applied myself. He felt that I was underutilizing my potential and encouraged me to go back to school. He observed that I was a quick study and was highly intelligent, so he was ready to help me to further my education. He was driven and studious himself, being a student in a tertiary institution. He provided me with funds for my books and made sure that I lacked nothing. I remember once when I fell ill and was admitted at the hospital; at that time, he was supposed to purchase some handouts for an upcoming examination, but he instead used that money to pay off my hospital bills and supported me until I was fully recovered. I was grateful for his attention, kindness and care, but within me I was confused. I did not know the difference between love and friendship; neither did I know whether I loved him or not. I did not know how to express my feelings through words or actions. I also did not know how a girlfriend was supposed to behave or what he required or expected of me in the relationship. I was green and innocent, and I was also emotionally immature. I believe that he had initially thought that I was mature beyond my age. Because I was seen on billboards and TV screens all the time, people felt that I was a promiscuous person; but in reality, I was the exact opposite.

In most of our visits, he would talk, and I would listen; yet he kept coming back. He was genuinely trying to help me to progress in life, but to me, he was way too nice. I was suspicious that he was not sincere because I had never had anyone treat me with such care and kindness. I had all my defenses up at all times, and could not open up to him. The wounds I had sustained in my young life were still fresh, and psychologically I was not ready yet for that kind of a relationship. By the time I realized that he genuinely loved me and that I also loved him, it was too late. He had gotten fed up with my indifference and moved on. I do not blame him because he did all he could and bent over backward to make our relationship blossom. Soon after he walked away, he found someone else. I stayed away out of respect for him; and though it hurt, I had to watch him leave. Later on, we reconnected and forged a strong friendship. And though we live far apart, he checks on me to be sure I am still on track with pursuing my dreams. He has expressed his hopes for our children to meet and play together one day. He was one of the few people who saw the potential in me and actively supported me.

By the age of twenty-two, I had learned that when someone was showing me love and care, I needed to reciprocate it. With this bit of understanding, I decided to give love another chance, so I entered into my second relationship. I met my second boyfriend through my boss, Mr. Omari. We went to perform at an event, and afterward, a gentleman walked up to my boss and told him that he was interested in me. My boss then went ahead and made the introductions. We started off as friends, and then progressed into something more. I was determined to make this relationship succeed because I did not want it to end up like the first one. So I gave it my all; I gave him more attention, showed him more love and did all I could to please him. I cooked, cleaned and was always at his beck and call. I took care of his every imaginable need. In my way of thinking, I had to do all the things that I had not done in my first relationship; otherwise, I would lose him like I lost my first boyfriend. Also, this man was a celebrity who had women throwing themselves at him wherever he went. He was ambitious and focused on maintaining and building his stardom status so much so that he barely gave me the attention I craved for, even though he continually professed his love for me.

One day I came to a realization that I could be jealous and possessive. As the saying goes, a jealous woman investigates better than the CID! I went ahead and did a thorough investigation on my boyfriend and found out that he had numerous other girlfriends apart from me. To make matters worse, he had a long-standing relationship with another woman who claimed to be his fiancé. When I confronted him with my suspicions, he did not seem to care, and because of that, we ended up arguing ever so often. I began to wonder whether this was a relationship I wanted to continue to invest in. He continued to cheat on me and broke my heart. He made me shed many tears, until one day the last straw broke the camel's back. One evening, I showed up at his house unannounced only to discover a woman there. On seeing me, she must have guessed that I was one of the man's women, so she attacked and fought me until I almost lost my life. In a rage, she broke a bottle and tried to stab me with it! Later on, I found out that she had invested many years of her life into her relationship with the man and was obsessively possessive of him. After that horrific encounter, I felt that enough was enough, and that the relationship was not worth my life, so I walked away.

In hindsight, the interesting thing about this man was that he liked listening to my advice and encouragement, especially where his career was concerned. I also believe that he must have loved me in his own way because there were moments when he was tender with me and behaved like he cherished me. He even had my name tattooed on his hand; but he was a womanizer and a Casanova, and that, I could not tolerate. So this time around, I had given out my all but ended up in the mud. This relationship drained me so much that I stayed away from men and did not enter into any relationship for several years.

Later on, I understood why my relationships had not stood a chance. Love without God is empty and vain. Love without God is usually conditional and manipulative. It does not go beyond sex and transient sensations. When beauty and sensations fade, this kind of "love" fades away with it. Only love tempered with the unconditional love of God can truly have meaning and last the test of time.

"Passion will warm you for days, infatuation will warm you for months, but love will set you on fire for a lifetime." — Matshona Dhliwayo

Chapter Seven

Adventures in Japan

**Behold, I am with you and will keep
you wherever you go, and will bring you
back to this land; for I will not leave you
until I have done what I have spoken
to you." —Genesis 28:15 (NKJV)**

I was part of a group of dancers and vocalists
who were in demand by most of the musicians
around. They wanted us to work and travel with
them outside the country for their shows. However,
they could not afford to pay for our expenses, so we
had to pay for our own way. Unfortunately, since I
never had enough money, I was always left behind.
So time and time again, I had to stay behind and
watch my friends go off with some of the musicians
to different parts of the globe. I did not allow this to
discourage me but continued to do my best where
I was, under the circumstances. But one day, my
endurance paid off; a man called Mr. Stone came
to Ghana in search of some good dancers, hair-
dressers and vocalists to go to Japan as contract
workers. As I had experience in all these fields, I
decided to try my luck by auditioning.

To my great delight, I was chosen to travel with
the team! With excitement, I started to prepare for

this new adventure. My great-grandmother and Pastor Joe lent me some money. Everything went smoothly except for the harrowing process of going through the interviews for a visa. The officials at the Japanese embassy were suspicious of me because according to them, I did not look like a Ghanaian. My fair skin color, the long length of my hair, and my narrow nose were the culprits. I had to speak in three different Ghanaian dialects and had to interpret the meaning of my name to convince them that I was genuinely Ghanaian before they finally approved me. What sealed the deal was when I interpreted my surname at their request. God, who foresees everything, saw it fit to give me a last name which means "Everyone is going." Somehow that touched my interviewer, and he stamped my visa! Over a thousand people applied for a visa, but they were all denied except for three of us! Words cannot describe the immense joy and wonder that flooded my soul when I was handed my visa. With tears of joy streaming down my face I beamed at the world. Finally! I felt like my life had just been elevated to another level, and I was about to enter into an experience I had never had before. That day I learned a valuable lesson: that God has a good plan for our lives, and we do not need to rush ahead of Him. In due season, He will make things happen beyond our wildest dreams. In His own time, He makes all things beautiful.

My great-grandmother was beside herself with joy and thanked God for giving me this opportunity of a lifetime. We had ninety days to prepare for the trip, so I packed with excitement. I even packed "Gari" (a grain made from Cassava) and "Shito" (a spicy sauce made from dried fish and shrimps). I was fortunate to have a little pocket money with me. After saying all my goodbyes, I made my way to the airport, my heart beating fast with pure excitement. As we drove, I had a flashback to some years before when Pastor Joe was about to travel abroad. I went to see him off at the airport, and as we stood waiting for him to board the plane, I felt in my heart that one day I would also board a plane and travel abroad. Looking through the large glass windows, I stared at the airplanes flying in the air and prayed that God would open the door for me to also fly one day, no matter whether my destination was within the country or abroad. I just wanted to soar in the skies one day! While I was caught up in my thoughts, Pastor Joe walked up to me and said, "Don't worry my child, this is going to be your life-style. I know the reason why I brought you to the airport to see me off. Come and let me pray for you." He held my hands and shared a word of prayer with me, after which he told me that this would not be our last meeting. He advised me to hold on to my faith and continue to trust and obey God and His Word. That day I received an impartation from my mentor to travel and to soar in the skies. From that day onward, I never stopped dreaming. So finally, I stood at the airport, waiting to board the plane to Japan. I leaned against a wall, while the people bus-tled around me to and fro. I hopped onto Memory Lane once again and remembered how as a child I saw airplanes in the sky and waved excitedly at them, promising myself that one day I would sit in one. I slipped back to reality, praying that God would give me success and would not let me come back empty-handed. Finally, I boarded the plane and settled down in my seat. I pinched myself to make sure that I was not dreaming! Finally, we took off, and I was surprised that the intense vibrations and the roar of the jets did not alarm me. It almost felt natural to me, as though I had done it before. I settled back into my seat, relaxed and enjoyed the long trip to Japan. I looked down at the beauty of the handiworks of God. The landscape and the aerial views were breath-taking. I marveled at how tiny the buildings and cars looked from above. I was in awe at the beauty of the clouds. Transiting through Egypt, we were given an opportunity to tour a bit of the capital. The Egyptian cuisine was delicious; their women were beautiful, and the people were very hospitable.

Finally, we arrived in Japan and were warmly received. We were immediately given a contract to sign. We were not given a chance to even read it thoroughly, so we just signed it and went to our place of residence, which they had prepared for us in advance. It was when we were in the comfort of our rooms that we got a chance to read through the contracts that we had signed. Then it dawned on us that it was completely different from what we had agreed on before the trip.

On our first day of work, I met all kinds of people from Russia, Liberia, the Philippines, Ukraine and many other countries. We got acquainted and made small talk, and then we were asked to perform our welcome dances. Each day, we were taken to a theatre to rehearse until we became extremely competent entertainers. We entertained people during their festivals and were invited to perform at important events. After each performance, we were taken to a room where we educated people about Africa. As the days went by, we realized that our agents were not paying us the money that they had been given to pay us. I decided to confront one of them, stating unequivocally that I wanted to return to Ghana because of their breach of our contract and the unfair treatment they were giving us. I told them that I felt like I was in prison, so I wanted to go back home. My confrontation had its desired effect because soon after, our salaries were increased.

After a while, the patronage of our African dances waned, and the language barrier was making it difficult for us to communicate with others; even with our colleagues in the hostel. Though many of the Japanese could speak English, they never did, opting instead to speak their indigenous languages. Some of them pretended not to understand English to motivate us to learn the Japanese language. In spite of the challenges, I fell in love with Japan. I loved their colorful culture, music, and delicious food. They were a people who loved each other and gave valuable pieces of advice to those of us from other countries. Gradually I became fluent in the Japanese language, even though I used it to communicate for the duration of our six month stay. Life was not easy, as we were responsible for our own upkeep. To complement my income, I braided hair a couple of times but mostly focused on my dancing.

Tragically, some of my colleagues were so caught up in making as much money as they could that they got involved in prostitution, lesbianism, and drugs. There were nights when I would see some of them sneaking some old Japanese men into the hostel. Other nights I could hear the sick sounds of their illegitimate copulations, but I remembered all that Pastor Joe had taught me and vowed never to lower myself to adopt such a base lifestyle. And by the grace of God, I held onto my principles, kept myself and did not compromise my standards. I lived modestly and saved my money to invest in something lucrative when I returned to Ghana. I was able to send some money home to settle all my debts and paid all the interests on the loans as well. I was also able to send some money back to my great-grandmother and the salon for the upkeep of my apprentices. Things were going reasonably well until I started having some problems with some of my female colleagues.

The cattiness of some of the women started coming out, and envy began to manifest in them. Some of them gathered and gossiped about me. I was the victim of backbiting and false accusations. Even my Ghanaian colleagues who I considered to be like my family ganged up on me and betrayed me. They thought I was proud and full of myself because I was not getting involved in their mess. I also had issues with two ladies from Russia and Ukraine. They were called Christine and Anya, and they took us for granted. They worked and saved their money and sent remittances back home to their families, but they came and used our hard-earned resources and ate our food. Because they were Caucasians and they were dating some of the agents, they were given more opportunities while we, the black Africans were always sidelined.

What was even more troubling was that Christine, who was from Ukraine read tarot cards and was into palmistry. One day she asked me to allow her to read my palm. I rejected her offer and explained to her that I was a Christian and did not believe in sorcery and fortunetelling. I suppose that this offended her, so she got her friends to join her in rising up against me. One day she made the mistake of pilfering my food. After I politely asked her to give it back, she began to rant and rave. In spite of my small physical stature, I knew that I could beat her up without even trying. When she continued with her insults, I landed a nasty slap across her cheek and beat her up until she started begging for mercy. That taught her a lesson and ended her pilfering career! By the time I left Japan for Ghana, she had become one of my good friends.

Six months after I arrived, I was told that I could renew my contract, but by then I was done with Japan and was homesick, so I opted to return to Ghana. By this time, Pastor Joe had introduced me to a gentleman who lived in the United States. I had already received several marriage proposals back in Ghana. Pastor Joe counseled me not to rush into anything, but to pray about it and to take my time before committing to anyone. This gentleman from the States was so interested in me that he decided to meet me in Ghana once I had returned. After I packed my belongings and went back home to Ghana, he followed through and made the trip home. We met each other and became good friends without progressing beyond that. I settled down and began to strategize for the future.

Travel to learn character. — Julia Pardoe

Chapter Eight

Family Frictions and Forgiveness

When Joseph's brothers saw him coming,
they recognized him in the distance. As
he approached, they made plans to kill
him. "Here comes the dreamer!"
they said. — (Genesis 37:18)

I made a fortune from all my hard work in Japan, and it was now time for me to use the money judiciously. I prioritized my spending and decided to start out by sowing back into the lives of all those who had supported me up until then. Bearing gifts, I went around thanking all my supporters by giving them double what they had invested in me. I did not forget the old woman who used to encourage me when I was a little girl. I gave her an unusually large amount of money because I was so appreciative of what she had done for me when no one else cared.

By this time, God had done a work in my heart, and I was willing to forgive those who had hurt me. I went to thank them also, after I reasoned that had it not been for the pain they had caused me I would not have made it this far. It is not easy to come to that place of forgiveness, but when you look at the broader picture, you realize that those that hurt you drove you closer to God and empowered you to excel. Their rejection enabled you to discover your acceptance and value to God. The further they pushed you down, the harder and higher you climbed; the more they disdained you, the harder you worked. Never give up until you have proven your naysayers wrong and the counsel of God right. By doing so, you might win over to God those who trampled on you before. Do not allow bitterness to eat you up; release them, release yourself and move on. Out of bitterness, I once tried to take my life by drinking a whole bottle of kerosene. I thought that I would die and end it all, but death never claimed me because God still had work for me to do. I felt that all my dreams had ended, but it is not over until God says it is over.

"Don't think that just because you made it to the next level that the haters and naysayers disappear. Remember, new levels bring new devils."
—Steve Maraboli

After my "Appreciation Tour," I decided to expand my salon and open a supermarket for my family to run. Can you imagine? Me of all people, opening a supermarket for my family to run! Yes, I guess I am guilty of having a very big heart. So with my generous spirit, I launched my supermarket business and hired my family members to run it. The girl who started with a little table, selling Milo had certainly come a long way! So I asked an uncle and his wife to run the store. After a year, I realized that we were not breaking even; yet we were always running out of products. I suspected that they were not giving me accurate accounts, so I decided to confront them. They managed to reason their way out of it by giving me all kinds of excuses which I bought, hook, line, and sinker. They even convinced me to hide the fact that I was the true owner of the business and to allow them to be the face of the business to protect me from the "bad guys."

Once more, I restocked the shop, and as I was advised, left it entirely in their care. In less than six months, the shop went downhill once again, and I felt that it had become a money pit. I regretted ever going into business with a family member. By then, they had reverted back to the name-calling which I had suffered from as a child. I was told that I was the daughter of a "nobody" who had no right to teach them how to run "their" store; that I thought that just because I had gone to Japan, I could come back and become a boss over them. And still being the youngest in the family, they managed to rip me off and ran me out of my own establishment!

I thought that investing in my family would finally buy me their acceptance. I did not understand that this is a challenge that most people who have been rejected face. They unconsciously try to buy their family's acceptance by allowing them to use them to no end. Because they are so thirsty for love and acceptance, they end up bending over backwards to please the very people who are trying to kill them. I was still innocent, so I wondered what I had done wrong to deserve such a dreadful treatment. So with heaviness of heart, and kicking myself for putting myself in a position to be betrayed by family once again, I washed my hands entirely off the store and walked away.

With that done, I decided to focus my attention on expanding my salon so that I could recruit more people to train. I had the building reconstructed, extended and refurbished until it had doubled in capacity and size. I also had a vision of building a school beside the salon. I told my great-grandmother about my vision, which she believed was a good one. So she gave me one piece of her land after she had gone to see the chief of the town, along with an uncle, my brother and a few trusted friends of hers as witnesses. I finally became the owner of the land, broke ground and started to build. Sadly, a few months afterwards, my great-grandmother passed away. This was a massive blow to me. Granted, over the years we had our ups and downs, but she was the most consistent figure in my life and had been my pillar throughout my life. Now, with her gone, I felt that I was really on my own. Her demise caused a rift in the family, as family members fought over her possessions.

During this time of mourning, I was told that the land on which I was building the school had been rented to another person, though the building at this time had reached its lintel level. According to the messenger, my building had been razed down and rebuilt as a rental property. And not only that; the person who had rented the land had vowed to have me killed if I ever set foot on the land. The shock of it all was almost too much for me to bear. What was I, a young, single woman to do? I heeded the warning and did not go near the land for years. Several years later, while I was on an errand, I happened to pass by the site and saw that a house had been put up for rent and had tenants living in it. I decided to approach one of the tenants and asked them whether they knew who owned the property. To my utmost surprise, the landlords were no other than my own relatives who my great-grandmother had requested to act as witnesses on the day that I had bought the land! Unknown to me, they had gone behind my back and had connived with an elder who was also present during the sale to take the property away from me. My jaw dropped! I was shocked and was utterly speechless. Was there no depth to which these people would sink? And all I wanted to do was to be a blessing to them! My sorrow knew no bounds. I thought to myself how sad my great-grandmother would be if she could see what the people she had trusted had done.

"To seek greatness is the only righteous vengeance."
— Criss Jami

Chapter Nine

Compassion:
A Lost Virtue

"It is mine to avenge; I will repay. In due time their foot will slip; their day of disaster is near, and their doom rushes upon them." —(Deuteronomy 32:35)

M y visions for the school were cruelly put on hold, and it took me a long time to recover from the betrayal of my family. It still puzzles me how cruel people can be, and how they can so easily maltreat the downtrodden without any remorse. Anytime I hear stories similar to mine, my heart breaks. Street people and the less privileged are always looked down upon and denigrated. Let us remember what the Bible says in Psalm 118:22, *"The stone that the builders rejected has now become the cornerstone."* The one you are harassing might end up becoming your lifeline. Let us be mindful of how we treat the orphans, the homeless, the deaf and dumb, the blind, and the disabled. We are all the apples of God's eye and a person that maltreats anyone that is weaker than himself sets God against him and invites His contention.

Deuteronomy 32:35 says, *"It is mine to avenge; I will repay. In due time their foot will slip; their day of disaster is near, and their doom rushes upon them."* I did not wish it upon them, but those who paid my good with evil died one after another within the span of two years. It was almost as though they were on a hit list and were being eliminated one by one. As soon as one died, the next person followed. It was very unsettling, but I chalked it up to one of the mysteries of life. However, I will always wonder whether this was due to just a series of coincidences or a performance of divine judgment.

Where is the love of God that is being preached all over in churches and on the streets? It baffles me how some Christians who seem to be so active and vocal in their churches, and are always taught about the love of Christ find it so easy to harm the less privileged without being remorseful in any way. Dare to go to the houses of some pastors, and you will be shocked to see how they and their wives treat their House Helps! How can they preach one thing and live the exact opposite?

And let us talk about the families from which these orphans, the blind and deaf come. How can the extended family watch them suffer and not even feel any compassion for them? They insult and abuse them at the least provocation. They watch them go hungry; and force them to do the most demeaning chores. Sometimes they rape them, and then on Sundays, they go to church and dance and praise God. This is the picture of human depravity, and those who wallow in it do not know God. Throughout generations, House Helps have always been at the bottom of the totem pole. If we really want to be honest, they are actually slaves. They are stripped off their living rights and are sometimes raped; and if the act should result in pregnancy, they are forced to have abortions which some of them do not survive. Just one of them can be forced to have more than five abortions in one home, after which they are fired and sent out into the world to fend for themselves. Their families in the village do not want them back because they are an extra mouth to feed. So they end up on the streets, sometimes going as far as to enter into prostitution. If they are not fired, in worst case scenarios, they are poisoned and vanish off the face of the earth. These are true words, and not speculation; I lived it and saw it.

I am a voice to the House Help. Sometimes all they need is someone they can talk to and someone they can bare their hearts to. They need someone to embrace them and put a smile on their faces. They need someone to see the potential in them and feed the greatness in them that poverty has managed to suppress. They need some respect and need to be spoken to politely. Let us fear God enough to respect and have compassion for His children. Let us practice what we preach.

Do not take advantage of the widow or the fatherless. (Exodus 22:22)

Instead, we must *"Defend the weak and the fatherless; uphold the cause of the poor and the oppressed."* (Psalm 82:3)

James 1:27 says, *"Pure and genuine religion in the sight of God the Father means caring for orphans and widows in their distress and refusing to let the world corrupt you."*

Psalm 146:9 also says, *"The LORD watches over the foreigner and sustains the fatherless and the widow, but he frustrates the ways of the wicked."*

The Bible speaks of how dear to God's heart are the downtrodden and the weak. It also talks about the penalties that are lined up for those who treat the less fortunate in an unworthy manner. God is watching, and He will defend His people! Politicians, it is my humble plea that you should seriously consider these issues at hand and come out with policies that will protect the less fortunate. Creating training centers to give them a trade could go a long way in setting them up for a brighter future. Please put the nations' resources to good use and do well to remember us. Put us also on your priority list. The blessings of God are extended to the generous and those with integrity. God has given you a platform for a reason. Use it in a manner that will please Him, and He will reward you. Material blessings and inner peace and joy abound towards those who extend their hands towards others. Long life and blessed descendants are rewards to the kindhearted.

I am not in any way judging or condemning the prosperous; instead, I'm trying to awaken their consciousness and compassion concerning these issues. It is my prayer that we will all sow into the lives of those around us who need a helping hand. There is a reason why God blesses people with wealth, and one day He will ask them to give an account of all that they did with the blessings He gave them. Just imagine if everyone were to look through their own family and select and show some kindness to a poor niece or nephew, how that could go a long way in making this world a better place. What a beautiful thing it would be if we could all demonstrate unconditional generosity, with no strings attached to those who have nothing.

House Helps are not only girls and young women; some are boys and young men. On the streets, I heard of how some of the boys came to adopt homosexual lifestyles because the men in the houses sexually abused them. And when a relative chose to take them through school, they would ask for sex in return. These are not tales; these are real atrocities that take place! If you were to hear some of the stories as I heard from the street children, you would mourn.

On the brighter side, to those who in their own little way are helping the less fortunate, just as my great-grandmother tried to do even though she herself was destitute, God richly bless you. It is my prayer that God will continue to bless and provide for you so that you can keep doing what you are doing. May God answer you whenever you call out to Him.

Now to my own people, the street children and house helps; the fact that you are on the streets does not mean that you cannot do anything for yourselves. I have been there; and yes, I was almost raped at times, but I resisted and overcame my attackers. I was even fired because of my defiance and was tossed out with just the clothes on my back, but I did not die; I persevered and endured. In this generation, there are many more opportunities out there than there were in my time. Never be brainwashed into thinking that you have to sell yourself, cheat or steal to make it out of poverty. I never gave in to any acts of immorality or social vices to get to where I am today. I worked hard and kept myself and most importantly, I trusted God, and He did not fail me. I am who I am today, because I worked hard with fierce determination to reach this height, and you can do the same too. Do not ever settle for less. Pray to God and have faith in Him to birth something beautiful out of your life.

I want to also advise the house helps to be careful in the way in which they comport themselves. There have been many cases in which some generous relatives have taken them in and lived to regret it. This is because with time, instead of their wards showing them gratitude, they have ended up becoming proud, lazy, and stubborn, and on some occasions have even stolen from them. It is unthinkable how some of us behave! Let us be mindful of our behavior and be gracious to our guardians and employers.

Charity is the matter of the heart and not of the pocket. — Swahili Proverb

Chapter Ten

More Crazy Adventures

***Behold, I am with you and will keep
you wherever you go, and will bring you
back to this land; for I will not leave you
until I have done what I have spoken
to you." — Genesis 28:15 (NKJV)***

A few years went by, and I met an air hostess who
became a very good friend of mine. She worked
with the "Fly Emirates Airlines." She used her
employee privileges to give me a great time and took
me to accompany her on many trips. Through her,
I was able to visit many countries. Sometimes she
would fly me over to join her for vacations wherever
she happened to be. Dubai was one of our favorite
places to visit, and I enjoyed those trips immensely.
Apart from the VIP treatment I received on the plane,
I spent some of my holidays in a seven-star hotel
with my friend and her crew. I enjoyed sight-seeing
at the famous Dubai Aquarium and other beautiful tourist sites. On my way back home from these
trips, my friend would go shopping for her family
and would send the items to them through me. As
I packed the things she gave me, I was intrigued by
the beautiful clothes that she included in her parcel.
I was inspired to try my luck in the fashion business, so I invested in high-end apparel. Although

things in Dubai were generally expensive, they were beautiful and unique. So I purchased some of the clothes, took them to Ghana and sold them to people who were interested in them, and I allowed them to pay them off monthly. Soon, I was shopping for bankers, government ministers and many others who paid generously for their deliveries by the end of each month. This made me travel to Dubai more frequently, depending on the needs of my clients until I was averaging a trip to Dubai every three months. After a couple of months of undertaking this business venture, my air hostess friend went on leave, and as time went by, we lost contact altogether. With the sudden cessation of my travel perks, it was difficult for me to afford to continue flying to Dubai. To sustain my momentum, I transitioned into retailing in Chinese products. With that, I launched a business which I named "The MBA Empire." I sold cosmetics, provisions, shoes, and clothes; a bit of everything, depending on what was in demand and what was available. I also took orders from soon-to-be-married couples and went around some African countries in search of what they needed for their nuptials. This provided me with a steady income for many months.

I frequented Nigeria where I bought lace materials, and "weave-on" hair products and wigs. In Abidjan, I bought jewelry and body lotions. In Togo, I invested in other textiles, provisions, copper chains and earrings. Travelling to these countries for business was an adventure which provided me with no shortage of exciting experiences. The first day I arrived in Togo, the next morning I woke up at dawn and dressed to blend in with the natives. I stuffed my money in my socks, and tied some around my waist.

Then I went for a long and relaxed stroll along the bustling roads of the capital city of Lomé. In Togo, I needed to be fluent in the "Ewe" language, which was one of their indigenous languages. There, the sun scorches far hotter than in Ghana. Sometimes when it became too hot for me to walk outside, I braved it and hopped onto a motorbike taxi, and off I would go to the nation's biggest market which was known as "Ashigame."

I was very frugal with my capital and had to be on top of the currency exchange to receive the best bang for my buck. This determined whether my trip would be profitable or not. For me, failure was just not an option, so I was very diligent and spent strategically. One of the most enjoyable aspects of my trip was in feasting on the Togolese cuisine, particularly "Adowe" a dish made of beans and "gari." My favorite drink was the pawpaw juice. After a hard day's work, when I was ready to set off back home, I would arm myself with all of my favorite foods. They consisted of "jolly kaklo," (a kind of doughnut made from corn); the sweetest "abolo," (a kind of dumpling made from corn dough); "ayigbe" biscuits, made from cassava starch and coconuts; and "tsofi" (fried turkey tail). I enjoyed my scrumptious food on the long journey back home, while I strategized on how to sell my goods. Sometimes I stayed for days, and other times I stayed for weeks, depending on what I came in to purchase. I became friends with many of the natives, and as time went on, I was given goods on credit because of the trust I had built with them. After purchasing the goods, I had to entrust them into the hands of certain individuals who specialized in shipping the products back home for lower duties. It was always a risky undertaking because sometimes the goods were stolen by some unscrupulous individuals. This was a collaboration of people who networked from different African countries. Going back home was also risky, as the vehicles could break down due to inadequate maintenance; or worse, armed robbers could attack us on the road. But by God's grace none of these evils befell me, and I went back and forth in safety.

One of the most rewarding aspects of my trips was learning the French language. I wasn't exactly fluent in it, but I learned enough of it to communicate intelligently with the people. I learned simple statements like, "Bonjour" "Comment vas tu?" "Je t'aime." "Je t'aime aussi." and "Tu es belle." When it came to bargaining with the traders, I said, "C'est combien?" "C'est trop chere." "S'il vous plait reduisez le prix." and "Je vous donnerai." It was an excellent experience for me

You were born to win, but to be a winner you must plan to win and expect to win. —Zig Ziglar

One day on a flight back home from Dubai, I sat next to an elderly man from Cote d'ivoire. Since I loved to sit by the window, I implored him to change seats with me, and he agreed. Soon, we began a conversation and got to know a little bit about each other. As we chatted, he told me not to underestimate the African market and to explore my business options within the continent. So after I got home, I did some research and decided to invest in body lotions and jewelry in Cote d'Ivoire. Thankfully, my business catapulted to another dimension after my first five trips.

Because I benefited so much from the advice that the old man gave me, I decided to search for him when I got back to Abidjan so that I could thank him. Upon reaching the airport, and armed with the contact information the man had given me earlier, I found his business which was on the airport premises. When I got there, I asked the receptionist whether I could use her phone to make a call. She asked me who I was looking for, and after I told her about the gentleman, she indicated that she worked for him. She was interested in knowing how I came to be acquainted with him. According to her, he was extremely wealthy and owned many gas stations. He was also a Muslim and had many wives. I was given a seat in the lobby and waited for him to show up. When he finally arrived, he rolled out the red carpet and gave me a VIP treatment. His receptionist brought me some refreshments while I waited for him to finish his work. Don't ask me how, but my instincts told me that the poor soul had a crush on me. I must confess that he was very handsome and attentive, neatly dressed and soft-spoken. He took me on a tour of the airport, and we were able to communicate quite well in French.

He coaxed me to stay a little longer, so I agreed. Later on in the evening, the man sent his driver to come and pick me up and take me to his house in town. On reaching his home, which was far away from the airport, I was flabbergasted at the sheer size and opulence of his mansion. I panicked, as I suddenly remembered that I had not told anyone about my whereabouts. I became more alert and conscious of my surroundings. My instincts were telling me that something was not quite right. While still seated in the car, I cautiously took in my surroundings.

As I was turning my head this way and that, I saw someone approach us on a motorcycle. As it got to the car, as if in slow motion, the person took off his helmet, and low and behold, it was not a man like I thought it was; it was the receptionist from the airport!

Suddenly the main gate to the mansion flung open, and we zoomed into the driveway of the house. As I was escorted to the Living Room, I noticed that the house was full of children. Some were sitting on the floor while others played around the house, and they all looked alike. Then there were the women! Women of all sizes and ages were scattered around the public area of the house. Most of them were in similar wrappers. They bowed to me speaking in French. They said to me, "Je vous en prie belle demoiselle." (Meaning, "You're welcome, beautiful young lady.") Then together they emptied the room and went elsewhere while chattering in the Hausa language.

In about ten minutes, a young lady escorted me to a room, where a huge calabash stood on the floor. She bowed and gestured to me, indicating that she wanted to wash my feet. The hair on the back of my head stood on end, as a shiver ran through my body. I got an eerie feeling and almost turned red with fright. I wondered whether this was some kind of a ritual she intended to perform on me. The lady, realizing that I was on the verge of hyperventilating, rushed out to tell the man about the situation. He swiftly came to where I was, and I lost no time in telling him that I was not feeling comfortable in the house. So he allowed me to gather my belongings and drove me to a hotel which was a bit closer to town. It was in the less desirable section of the city, with lots of people milling about and engaging in all kinds of activities. We left the man in the car while his driver escorted me to my room. I took a shower and got ready for bed, but for about an hour or two I struggled to fall asleep, all the while wishing that I was safely back home. Unfortunately, there was no way I could fly home that night because I did not buy a return ticket. What kept me awake were the sensual sounds that were coming through the thin walls of the rooms next to mine. The atmosphere was thick with perversion, and I could hear all kinds of ungodly sounds throughout the night. I felt incredibly vulnerable; like a sitting duck, even though my door was locked. As I considered my precarious predicament, I suddenly heard a knock on my door! Initially, I could not determine whether it was coming from my door or next door. So I looked through the peephole only to discover the old man standing there!

I wondered to myself, "What on earth is this man doing here at this hour?" So I opened the door by a little crack, and without even waiting for him to speak, I quickly announced to him that I appreciated him checking on me and that I was okay. Ignoring me, he pushed the door open, walked in and sat on the edge of the bed. He asked me whether I wanted something to eat, to which I quickly answered in the negative. Realizing how tense I was, he told me to relax. He took off his sandals and his long Muslim gown and tried to lie on my bed. I jumped up and almost lost it. I was terrified, and I thought to myself, "Did I manage to escape rape on the streets, only to end up here?" Then the better and stronger part of me took over, and I said to myself, "Calm down girl, you've got this." Then I did the smartest thing I could ever think of; I told a whopping lie! I asked him, "Please, are you a married man?" He responded with a French accent and said, "Don't worry Mommy, is fine, don't worry." As he said this, he stretched out his hand towards me, in a welcoming gesture. I suddenly broke into tears with loud groans as I cried out, "Oh no! Not again! No! Not again!" I said this over and over again in my Ghanaian dialect (Twi). I said to myself, "Tonight, either this man dies, or I die!" I repeated it so many times that he wanted me to interpret what I was saying, so I obliged. With a tear-stained face and a shaky voice, I told him that I was from a royal family and one of our taboos was that a royal woman was not allowed to sleep with a married man. And if that happened, the man, along with three of his family members would fall dead right after the completion of intercourse. My Oscar-winning performance seemed to have made its intended impact. The poor man's eyes almost bulged out of their sockets! Terrified, he jumped up from the bed and scurried around for his clothes. He shakily took out a couple of dollar bills and threw them on the bed, and was out of the room like a shot, without a backward glance! I locked the door firmly behind him, settled in the corner of the bed and I laughed myself silly, till tears of mirth flowed down my cheeks. I laughed myself to sleep!

Before the break of dawn, I was out of the hotel and on the way to the airport. I was in a hurry to make it to the safety of my home. A few months after I arrived back home, I went to the forex bureau exchanged the money he had thrown on top of the bed for cedis and gave it all to charity. Since then until now, I have never tried to swap seats with anyone on a plane; neither have I spoken to any strangers on a plane.

"Even from a foe, a man may learn wisdom."
— Greek proverb

Chapter Eleven

The Fulfilling of Purpose

**But Jesus looked at them and said to
them, "With men this is impossible, but
with God all things are possible."
—(Matthew 19:26)**

One day, a friend of mine who was a beauty queen invited me to have lunch with her at a restaurant near the Ghana Broadcasting Corporation, known as "The Honey Suckling." As we ate, three men walked over to our table. She excused herself and went a little distance away to talk to them. The next day, she called me on the phone and spoke to me about a project that she was involved with in Nigeria which had to do with orphans. She had to make a trip to Nigeria and asked me to accompany her. She said it was an all-expenses-paid trip, and all I needed to do was to show up. Since charity is my heartbeat, I did not hesitate and agreed to accompany her. We met at the airport, boarded our flight and after an uneventful trip, we arrived safely in Nigeria.

A car was waiting to pick us up at the airport, and we were whisked off to Ogba, which is in the Eastern part of Nigeria in River State. I took in the sights and admired the beauty of the city as the driver whisked us off to a big house which was privy to some fantastic views of the sunset. After taking in all the luxurious details of our surroundings, I asked my friend whether we were in the right place. She smiled and reassured me that this was our destination. For some reason I felt unsettled, but I tried to calm myself down. I was surprised to see only three people in the sprawling mansion: an elderly woman, a house-help and the owner of the house who was one of the gentlemen that had previously met us at the restaurant in Ghana. I was a bit confused because we had come purposefully to do some charity work, so I wondered what we were doing in the house, but I kept my queries to myself. After we had exchanged a few pleasantries with our hosts, my friend and I were escorted to our separate rooms.

Later on in the day, the owner of the house took us to one of the finest restaurants in Nigeria. I ate heartily, as the food was delicious! Spicy snails with rice, rich "Palaver" sauce with "Agushie" stew and "Eba" were all lined up before us, sending off a mouth-watering aroma. My previous confusion and trepidation seemed to evaporate with each delectable bite! We ended up spending a long week in Nigeria.

Throughout our stay, each time we met our host, he called me "Eshi." (I later on found out that this means a beautiful horse.) I was not sure where all this was going, but I did not have long to find out. One evening, the man asked us to dress up for a night out. During our outing, I realized that he was flirting with me, often smiling and being extra attentive to me. When we got back to the house, the man escorted me to a quiet place and proposed to me. To say that I was caught off guard would be an under-statement! Was it even possible for a person to offer marriage to someone he had just met? I wasted no time in telling him that I barely knew him and could not possibly accept his proposal. Being a gentleman, he told me that he would be patient and would give me time to get to know him a little better. From that evening until the day we returned to Ghana, I was treated like a queen by my suitor and his family, which included his mother and sisters. They treated me as though I was one of them and made me feel very much at home. It was apparent he had said something about me to his family, but I was still curious to find out about what he had told them, so I asked my friend. She told me that according to the man, it had been love at first sight; that from the minute he laid his eyes on me, he told her that I was the woman of his dreams. I was a bit skep-tical about that, but I decided to wait and see how things would unfold.

All too soon, we completed the project and our trip was over. A day before our departure, I overheard my suitor in an argument with his mother. Throughout our stay, I had never heard anything like that, so I was curious to know what had precipitated the shouting match. It was not until a few months after we had returned to Ghana that my questions were answered. It turns out that my friend who invited me to Nigeria became envious of me upon seeing how much the man liked and pampered me. So she went behind my back and told his mother some strange things about me, which generated the heated argument between him and his mother. I could not believe how duplicitous people could be! However, upon our departure, I was given lots of luxurious textiles and lace materials from the man's family which I began to wear in Ghana. Each time I had a piece made into a dress and wore it, I received lots of compliments. Predictably, that inspired me with another business idea, and with that, I went into the selling of Nigerian lace. It turned out to be a very profitable venture, and though it caused me to make many trips to Nigeria, I never got back in touch with the man.

As I went about travelling, I had a significant amount of clothes piled up which I no longer needed. So I decided to distribute them to people that I thought would appreciate them. I was gratified to see how grateful they were for those clothes. Their smiles and excitement proved how much they valued the garments. Some of the ladies were so excited that they folded the clothes and used them as pillows to be sure that they were not stolen. After observing this, I told myself that if my used garments could make such an impact on others, I had to do more. So I went a bit further and bought some second-hand clothes at the Kantamanto Market. I added them to my stash of garments and prepared to give them out to charity. I also went boldly from door to door, asking people to donate their old clothes for the less privileged. My efforts paid off, and I managed to gather a lot, which enabled me to make my very first donation to an orphanage in Darkuman, a suburb of Accra. It was a huge donation, which the children received with great joy. There were migrant children from all over West Africa. Handing the clothes out to them proved to be a tricky business. The children were so eager to get their clothes that they crowded and jostled us, shouting and laughing. I felt delirious with joy and amazement as I thoroughly enjoyed the warm hugs and the feeling of belonging. I could not get enough of those precious children, so I spent the entire day with them.

I was so hooked on the children's love that from then on, I did more investigations to find more orphanages around the country that I could give to. I started to pursue them, visiting the children's homes even when I had nothing to give. I went there, hoping to be of help to them in any way I could. Sometimes I would encourage the children or just be a listening ear to them. They were glad to share their stories with me, some of them so similar to mine. I went back into the business of selling wigs and cosmetics just to make more money to support my philanthropic efforts. Unfortunately, some of the homes turned me away, saying that I was just too young to make any meaningful contribution to their establishment. But I was unstoppable and driven, so I persevered until I won them over with the sheer volume of my donations.

My second significant donation was to the Cocoa Clinic in Accra. There were a lot of disabled children there who had come from all over the country to learn trades in shoemaking, bag-making, and sewing. Most of them though they were crippled in their limbs were extremely active in their minds. They were full of dreams and visions. Some of them were talented singers but had no one to appreciate their potential or to groom them. Some of the little girls said that they wanted to be princesses, while some of the boys said that they wanted to become presidents. Some of them were so handicapped that they could barely feed themselves. As I watched them struggle to lift their spoons to their mouths,

I felt like weeping. I felt a flood of gratitude flow through me as I thanked God for blessing me with good health in spite of all that I had suffered as a child. The caretaker to child ratio was low, and the children, who were frustrated, took it out on the caretakers. They became tough to handle, especially with their handicaps. The home was understaffed and they needed all the help they could get. I asked them how I could be of help to them after I donated some money to them. One day I had an epiphany. I got some of my apprentices to volunteer to go and teach some of the children hairdressing. So for three months, they labored with the children and poured out into them knowledge and skills. This produced amazing results and brought great joy to them.

I continued my trek around the children's homes; and the more I visited them, the more I desired to do more for them. Within a short amount of time, I was able to make several donations to places like the Labadi Street Children's Outreach in Accra; the Edwenase Rehabilitation Center in Kumasi; the Accra Psychiatric Hospital; the New Horizon Special School; Children with Autism in Accra and the Light House Children's Home in Cape Coast. One of the most critical aspects of operating any form of charity is accountability. My donors wanted to see photographs and videos of the work I was doing, to let them see the impact that their donations were making in the lives of the children. However, some of these homes were so hostile to us that they banned us from recording or taking pictures on their premises. It is incomprehensible how people you are trying to help will erect obstacles to make it more difficult for you to help them! Some of the homes were suspicious of us trying to use them to make a name for ourselves. Some of them even dismissed us from their premises right after we had made our donations! I was tempted to become bitter and discouraged, but I persevered, attributing their poor behavior to ignorance.

With time, I was inspired to introduce free health screenings into our ministry to the poor. Through this, I was able to touch over five hundred lives, which included market women who had no idea that they were walking around like ticking time bombs. Some of them had chronic high blood pressure, yet had no idea. Through the screenings, many of them became more conscious of their health. With those who needed immediate medical attention, they were referred to the nearby hospitals and clinics. These free screenings were of great benefit to the people of Fadama; the Makola Market; the Darkuman Market; the Nyamekye Market; the Aveno; the Mercy Day and the Light House Orphanages in Cape Coast.

"You can give without loving, but you cannot love without giving." — Amy Carmichael

I did the charity work alongside my hairdressing business and had even more apprentices coming in from all over the country to be trained. At a certain point, I realized that I needed to upgrade my knowledge and skills, so I enrolled in school at the "Second Image International Institute" to acquire a certificate in beauty therapy. I then continued to study at the "Allure College" where I obtained a license as a beauty specialist. With these two certificates, I officially set up a school. I named it the "Anaya Education Complex" which I built above the salon. Since this school was for the needy, it differed from other for-profit institutions. I provided every-thing that a needy student would possibly require to enable them to fulfill their educational pursuits within the school. The expansion also included a hostel where I housed the students that came from afar. I also provided them with food and clothing. The school trained both young men and women in cosmetology. They graduated after three months of intense training with certificates in hand. I waived the tuition and registration fees, so the only require-ment for enrollment was the readiness to learn. By the grace of God, since its inception until now, the school has trained not less than two hundred people who have established themselves in the beauty industry both within and outside Ghana. I was thrilled when some of them named their children after me. It was the icing on the cake. It touched me to know that my legacy would live on in the lives of some precious children.

The school became like a family to the students. When a new student arrived, we immediately initi-ated them into the fold by giving them a nickname. Many of the students who came from the rural areas came in with little or no knowledge of personal hygiene, so I had to personally teach some of them how to clean themselves properly. Many of them did not even know how to launder their clothes, so they had to be taught. Being athletic, I felt it was vital for them to learn how to stay fit, so on days when we had a light workload, I would take them out to a park and we would have some athletic competitions. We competed in both indoor and outdoor games, as well as tournaments. The winners received cash prizes. The evenings were like parties; we gathered around, cooked and ate together. After dinner, we had what I called "Confession Sessions" where students were allowed to confess things that they had done behind my back. They were also encouraged to ask questions and receive counsel regarding anything that concerned them. We had a very open and informal culture in the school. We encouraged team work and got the work done. Most of the students were eager to please and impress me, so they gave it their all. The graduation ceremonies were my favorite part of the whole process.

The only time the students had to provide any funding was during the graduation ceremony. I pegged the amount to be raised by each student to be GHC500. They were allowed to collect donations from their friends, families, churches, and loved ones to enable them to set up their start-up salons. I recorded how much each person was able to raise, and at the end of the graduation ceremony, I presented it back to them. With each graduation came a sense of fulfillment that words cannot express. It established this knowledge in my heart that with God any vision can come to fruition. I built that school from nothing, and am still amazed that I actually managed to pull it off.

"Every child needs a champion." — Hillary Rodham Clinton

Chapter Twelve

We Bleed While We Lead

**So let's not allow ourselves to get
fatigued doing good. At the right time we
will harvest a good crop if we don't give
up, or quit. Right now, therefore, every
time we get the chance, let us work for
the benefit of all, starting with the people
closest to us in the community of faith.
— (Galatians 6:9-10)**

U sually, after enjoying the euphoria of the graduation ceremony, I am confronted by how much of my own money has gone into the cost of the event. I do not keep any of the funds raised by the students, and I also distribute the offerings that are taken during the ceremony to the graduates. Some of the parents of the graduates who come from the rural areas usually bring me gifts from their farms like cassava, plantain and vegetables. The students cook them and serve the visitors dishes like "fufu" and "ampesi." This whole effort is a complete labor of love, so I never keep anything for myself. My reward is in giving a chance to those who have none and seeing them excel in life. Just hearing the words, "God bless you" or "Thank You" was enough for me.

After the graduation ceremony, I asked some of the students to stay on to work for me. I took care of their lodgings and started them on a salary of GHC200.00. (This was known as the "work and pay" system.) For six months, they worked with me to enable them to receive more training and save more money towards their start-up businesses. Not all of those that I approached accepted my offer since they were in a hurry to go back to their villages and establish themselves in the industry. I was intentional in putting some structures in place which would enable them to leave peacefully. There were also others who wanted to "work and pay" but not with me. They preferred to acquire some more skills and broaden their experiences by working in other salons. I saw them all off properly with best wishes for their success. The few that chose to remain with me joined hands with me and worked with me in the main salon. The experiences I had with some of them would make a most riveting reality show!

The drama was unbelievable! The betrayals, thefts, lies, gossiping and other vices that took place nearly made me look elsewhere for help. Suddenly these students who initially came in looking docile and ragged forgot where they came from and became proud. Loyalty was extremely hard to find among the people that I had labored for, and this was very painful for me. When the hurt became overwhelming, I went down memory lane, remembering how some of their friends and families had begged me to take them in to train them. Some of them had been brought from mission trips and crusades in far-flung towns and villages. I fully fed, sheltered and trained them, yet they turned against me.

After doing this work for a couple of years, I found that there were five categories of apprentices. The first category was made up of people who came in without even the most basic sense of personal hygiene. They were the ones who ended up becoming promiscuous. The second category was made up of those who were docile, humble and patient on arrival. However, they bided their time throughout the duration of their training. After their graduation, they revealed their true colors. The third category was made up of students who were studious. They graduated successfully, but eventually became complacent and lazy and gave all kinds of excuses for their poor performance. The fourth category was made up of those who started off lazy and uncommitted but became successful professionals. They were the ones that stayed the longest with me, as compared to those who pretended to be hardworking and humble in the beginning. The fifth category was made up of trainees who became proud as soon as they had been able to learn how to perform a skill or two. After pride set in, they tried to compete with me because they thought that they had become better than me.

The drama did not end with the students but their families as well. When their wards were first admitted, the families were very submissive and attentive to what I had to say and fulfilled all the requirements I asked of them. After some time, however, their behavior changed. As soon as they realized their wards could stand on their own two feet, they convinced them to move back home to start working even before their graduation. Most of them succeeded in pulling their wards out prematurely, thinking that they were outsmarting me. They went away without graduating, with the confidence that they could establish themselves with the little that they had learned. Sometimes their cockiness grew to astronomical proportions, and they dared to fight me and threaten me in my own shop! Though it upset me greatly, I pitied them because I knew that there was no way they would go far in life with those kinds of attitudes. In some instances, some of these trainees who had left prematurely in pride, flopped and came back to apologize for what they had done. Some never came back to apologize out of shame, even though they knew that what they had done was wrong.

Apart from dealing with the issues with my trainees and their families, I had to also deal with the drama that surrounded my family! Operating a business in a family home is one of the most difficult things that anyone can do. They thought that I had forsaken them in favor of strangers (the trainees). Some of my relatives did all they could to shut my school down, and when they could not succeed, they turned some of my students against me. For some reason, my relatives had this strange idea that I had told my students that they were evil, so they incited their children against me. One day, some of my relatives stormed the salon and destroyed a lot of my property. Some of my students tried to win the favor of my family members, so went to them and gossiped about me and told them every-thing that went on in my business. They lied about me and divulged sensitive information that I had trusted them with. Some of my relatives in turn came and told me what my students had told them. These were some of the students that I trusted the most. Also, some other family members thought that I had brainwashed my students about them, so this also sparked a kind of rivalry between them. The least incident caused a major row, which led to my relatives sometimes insulting my trainees by calling them outcasts. This happened mostly in my absence of course. Sometimes my relatives came in to have their hair done, and when we charged them, they were offended. They were expecting us to do their hair for free because they were family members. Insecurity and inferiority complex manifested themselves in horrible ways through some of my family members. With all these things going on, there was never a day of peace in my business.

The chaos escalated to unbelievable proportions after I got married, relocated to the U. S. and left my business to some of my most trusted protégés. After the first few months of my relocation, I received news that they had taken all the proceeds from the business for themselves and squandered them. They broke our contract which stated that they could use a certain percentage of the proceeds for their personal expenses and leave the remainder for me. Apparently, they were influenced by their families and friends and were told that I was taking them for granted; that they deserved to establish something on their own. I was heartbroken; and my heart bled at their betrayal. Indeed, the love of money can make people behave atrociously.

My business had become a live soap opera! The plots were so complex that if they had been turned into a reality show, it would have won awards! One day, an elderly tenant in our compound managed to convince one of my girls to move from the hostel into her apartment so that she could carry on an affair with the woman's son. Eventually, the girl got pregnant and had the audacity to be rude to me when I confronted her. This is a girl that I brought all the way from Kumasi to Accra. She was so destitute she could not even afford her transportation to the school. I paid for her to come to Accra and taught her everything she knew until she became a very capable hairdresser. After her graduation, I hired her as a "work and pay" employee. Sadly, she became one of my greatest disappointments. She left my business and got employed in another salon, then stole their clients. Afterward, she found a spot in my family compound and set up her own salon, and managed to steal many of my clients as well. She competed with me like I was one of her classmates, and this caused a huge rift between us, but by God's grace, I managed to hold my peace. Once she had given birth to her baby, her boyfriend left her for another woman who he ended up marrying. He told her that she was an illiterate, and so he traded her in for a college graduate. She was so broken that she regretted her actions and came to plead with me for forgiveness. I told her that I had nothing to say to her, and so with that, she packed her bags and went back to her village in Kumasi.

Your rejection is the foundation for your election. —_Richard Branson_

My leaders who I had entrusted the work to ran it into the ground. I had to make a trip back to Ghana to straighten out all the mess that they had made in my absence. These were people that I had not only sown into financially, but spiritually as well. I took them to the Achimota Forest on a weekly basis where I taught them how to pray. I taught them the Word of God and tried to replicate the kind of mentoring that Pastor Joe had given me. I honestly did not expect anything from them in return. I knew in my heart that with the kind of charity work I was doing, I would go through some heart-breaking experiences, but nothing prepared me for the level of ingratitude, betrayal, and disloyalty that I saw. So when I returned to Ghana, I had my work cut out for me. I had just admitted a new batch of trainees to the school, but my leaders were in such a hurry to leave and set up their salons that they were not willing to stay behind to even see the new entrants through. There was nothing I could do than to release them and send them off. I did my best not to fault them, but it hurt. Among the bunch of bad nuts, there was, thankfully, one good one. She stayed behind and took care of the salon as well as the new entrants, but she ended up falling in love and wanted to get married. She began to pressure me. How could I keep her against her will? So, though it was a great loss to me, I had to let her go. She left after the last batch of trainees had graduated, and with that, the drama of that generation came to a close. If this batch of trainees had not managed to kill me, the next batch not only killed me but put nails in my coffin as well! Not only did they squander all the proceeds from the business, but they also sold the things in the salon. They made sure that everything I had toiled for throughout the years came to nothing. This new batch was also the laziest among all those that had come before them. I remember how I went shopping in the States for them. I bought some toiletries and clothes and shipped them. Imagine how sad I was when I heard that the students called my gifts rubbish; yet they wore these same clothes and boastfully modeled around in them. My relatives aided these girls in their traitorous actions, and by the time I returned to Ghana, I came to meet an empty salon. My relatives, particularly ones that I had helped in the past were happy to see me fail. They did not even try to hide their satisfaction when they saw that I had failed once again. Also, my brother, who I had asked to oversee everything in my absence also helped to squandered my money. When I went to the bank to check how much money I had left in my business account, I wept. I had left this last batch of leaders in charge for a whole year and came to find nothing in my account. It was a massive blow to me. Nonetheless, I still believed that the vision was not a man-made vision, but was a God-given vision, so I did not give up. I did not let it break me, though I was utterly discouraged. Instead, I rolled up my sleeves and prepared to rebuild.

"Successful people are always looking for opportunities to help others. Unsuccessful people are always asking, "What's in it for me?" — Brian Tracy

Chapter Thirteen

Perseverance

***Therefore take up the whole armor of
God, that you may be able to withstand
in the evil day,
and having done all, to stand.
—Ephesians 6:13-18 (NKJV)***

S o far, I have painted a somber picture, but thankfully, every cloud has a silver lining. There were
a few of the students that took my training seriously and humbled themselves enough to apply my
counsel. Today I am happy to report that they are
all excelling in their businesses both within Ghana
and overseas. After the last batch of students graduated, I was so drained and heartbroken by all the
betrayal and projections of ill-will against me from
my relatives that it took me quite a while to recover
emotionally from the hurt. I gradually progressed
towards wholeness, and by God's grace, I made it to
the point where I could intelligently plan, strategize
and put things in place. I went back to the drawing
board and rebuilt the school and the salon. I refur-
nished and finally reopened them and received a
new batch of trainees. This time I was extremely
vigilant, and I did not rest. I made sure that I was
fully involved in the minutest details concerning the
business. This meant that I had to be flying back

and forth from the States to Ghana several times throughout the year. My trust had been completely destroyed. If I could not trust my own relatives, who else could I trust? I trusted no one, but still I could not do the work alone.

Within a short period of time, I renamed the school "The Stacy Foundation." This time, I did not concern myself with the students' lodgings or their feeding. All my students had to make sure that they had relatives within the city that were ready to take them in; so all my trainees were day students. With everything back on track, I decided to partner with a good friend of mine who had graduated from the "Second Image Institute." After graduating, she was still unemployed, so I hired her as a teacher to train the apprentices. Thankfully this arrangement went well. After I was convinced that everything was firmly in place and it was safe for me to return to the States, I left. It was difficult for me to relinquish the reigns of my vision to another person once again. However, I hopefully took the risk and left everything in her care. Nothing would have convinced me that tragedy would strike again.

"A lion does not flinch at laughter coming from a hyena." — Suzy Kassem

Six months after I left for the States, this friend of mine that I had put in charge of everything turned against me. She somehow managed to run out all the students from the school, making up a strange story about how they would be better off finding another school. I still cannot understand how she managed to convince all the students to leave the school. She ultimately pulled down everything I had just rebuilt, and so within six months of reopening, I had to shut down the institute once again. Up until now, I cannot figure out how or why my friend did what she did, but I can only say that I know for sure that she never considered me to be her friend to start with. I believe that from the very onset she had determined to make sure that my vision would never succeed. This might be my hurt talking, but I reasoned that no genuine friend could have done what she did to me. She never showed any remorse, but I have made my peace with God about what happened.

Once again, I headed back home to Ghana in sadness and heaviness of heart. This time I did not return alone but had my three-month-old baby in my arms. As I sat on the plane, I wondered what I was going to do. There was no integrity left in this world. Trust had grown wings and flown away to another planet. Goodwill did not seem to exist anymore. I felt so sad that there was not a single person I knew that I could trust to partner with me in this great vision. What had this world come to? I know of so many Ghanaians who are abroad who are in a similar predicament. They have great ideas that would benefit their families, communities and the nation, but they have no one to trust back home to help them. It seemed like it was better to do business with a complete stranger than a family member. This is such a tragic state of affairs! Imagine what our African nations would be like if all of those abroad who had visions for their native countries could find trustworthy people to manage these enterprises for them!

So once again, I was back to square one. Since giving up is not in my nature, I had no other option than to try again. I psyched myself, rolled up my sleeves and tackled the mess that this lady had left in her wake. I went around and tracked down some of my trainees, repaired the lines of communication and convinced them to return to the school. Some of the students, on hearing that I had returned, came back of their own volition. I employed new leaders and revived the foundation. I managed to hire another teacher, who was also a graduate from "Second Image." She came to help with the tutorials every three months and gave off her best and received her salary at the end of the month. But I observed that she never really took to being in charge and was never fully vested in the foundation, but she got the job done. She did her job well enough that I grew to like her and we became good friends. We discovered that we had a lot in common; we were both married with children and had other similar interests. We were such good friends that we even shared some of our secrets with each other. However, it was later that I discovered that unknown to me she was stabbing me in the back by telling the students all kinds of lies and bad things about me. I do not know how long this betrayal went on, but I discovered it one day when an elderly employee called me on the phone. She told me that my friend had gone to ask her for some US dollars and had told her stories about how I did not have the students' or the teachers' interests at heart, and how I never paid them their full salaries. So with this story she was able to convince the elderly woman to lend her the money, which she gave her two weeks to repay. After the time was up, she tried to contact the woman to remind her that it was time to repay her loan, but she was nowhere to be found. What surprised me most was that a few days before the elderly lady told me all this, my friend had texted me over and over again, asking me to send her money, which I told her I did not have because I still had some goods that I needed to clear at the port.

According to the elderly woman, she would never have reached out to me on account of all the bad things my friend had told her about me. She was so disappointed by what she heard that she decided not to associate with me any longer. The only reason why she even called me was that there was money involved and she had to account for it. Once again, the person I had been kind to had repaid my generosity with evil. On one of my visits to Ghana, I had paid her three months' salary in advance, in the amount of GHC1000.00. Since it was during the Christmas season, I also shipped down some gifts, goods and high-end designer clothes to her to share among my workers. Due to the relationship we had, she went ahead and picked some of the clothes for her husband. She even told me later on that she returned the clothes because her husband did not like them. After she returned them, she picked out some new ones for him. These were no ordinary clothes; they were expensive clothes that I sold in my boutiques in the States. I shipped them with the price tags still on them. As if that was not enough, during graduation, some of the students' families brought me gifts. Since I was not there to receive them, I gave her the liberty of collecting and enjoying all my gifts. So, looking at all these things that I had done for her out of the affection I had for her, her betrayal truly shattered my heart. I was utterly devastated and never thought that I would recover from it. Yet, even after this, I did not give up. I employed some new teachers from the city of Kumasi and other surrounding towns. As soon as they got settled and established, they suddenly turned against me. I realized that this negative cycle was meant to discourage me and to stop me from dreaming, but failure is not in my dictionary. I am the kind of person that never quits until I win. I still have a long life ahead of me, and I have many more dreams and visions to bring forth. I am still standing! I am still making a difference in this world, no matter how small it may seem. This is what God created me to do; and each day I live and breathe to fulfill my calling in this life. God has blessed me abundantly. I started with absolutely nothing, but today I have more than I need and manage to bless those who are less fortunate. This is what gives me the greatest joy and fulfilment in life.

I have learned so many things in my young life. I have discovered that trustworthy people are rare and hard to find, and if you have even one person in your life that genuinely has your best interests at heart, you are truly blessed. I have also learned that a majority of human beings cannot be trusted, so my dependence and trust is in God and God alone. I have learned that as one who has been rejected, I need not buy the affections of others, but be content in who I am in Christ. I have also learnt that it is essential to have the discernment to perceive those around you; to know those who are pretenders and those who are really for you. I hope and believe that with time my perceptions about people will change for the better.

Yes, I am still growing, still learning and still healing; but I am still moving forward by the grace of God. I was despised, rejected, disowned and abused, but I am still the King's choice for His work on earth. He loved me, accepted me and made me His own. He lifted me out of the pit and gave me a platform. I owe Him my life. I look forward to my future with optimism and faith in Him. It is not by might, nor by power, but it is by His Spirit. So into my future I walk, with full confidence that my star and my light will continually shine in the darkness. Into my future I soar on the wings of the Spirit to the pleasant places that God has prepared for me. If I could make it this far, so can you. No matter where you are in life, or what you are up against, with Christ Jesus in your vessel, you can surely smile at the storm. You will not just survive; but you will thrive, because you are also the King's Choice!

Being confident of this very thing, that He who has begun a good work in you will complete it until the day of Jesus Christ. — (Philippians 1:6)

THE END

CPSIA information can be obtained
at www.ICGtesting.com
Printed in the USA
BVHW061929071019
560431BV00004B/147/P

9 781545 643204